Around the World

by Freighter

Around the World
by Freighter

DISCOVER YOUR WORLD FROM A CARGO SHIP

BOB HARTLEY

Note for Librarians: a cataloguing record for this
book that includes Dewey Classification and US
Library of Congress numbers is available from
the National Library of Canada. The complete
cataloguing record can be obtained from the
National Library's online database at:
www.nlc-bnc.ca/amicus/index-e.html
ISBN 1-4120-3227-X

Printed in Victoria, BC, Canada

TRAFFORD

**This book was published *on-demand* in
cooperation with Trafford Publishing.**
On-demand publishing is a unique process and
service of making a book available for retail sale
to the public taking advantage of on-demand
manufacturing and Internet marketing. **On-demand
publishing** includes promotions, retail sales,
manufacturing, order fulfilment, accounting and
collecting royalties on behalf of the author.

Suite 6E, 2333 Government St.,
Victoria, B.C. V8T 4P4, CANADA
Phone   250-383-6864
Toll-free   1-888-232-4444
Fax   250-383-6804
E-mail   sales@trafford.com
www.trafford.com/robots/04-1054.html

10   9   8   7   6   5   4   3   2   1

Dedicated to

My son Paul and his family

Pamela, Connor, and Kaitlin

and

My daughter Louise and her family

Douglas, Karen, and Susan

Treasure life's voyage

SCHOOL DAYS

CONTENTS

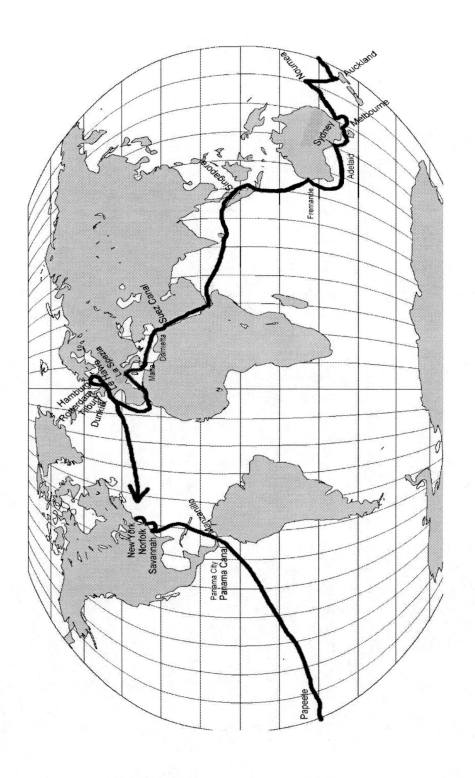

ITINERARY

1. New York, USA
2. Norfolk, USA
3. Savannah, USA
4. Manzanillo, Panama
5. Panama Canal Transit
6. Papeete, Tahiti
7. Auckland, New Zealand
8. Noumea, New Caledonia
9. Sydney, Australia
10. Melbourne, Australia
11. Adelaide, Australia
12. Fremantle, Australia
13. Singapore
14. Jeddah, Saudi Arabia
15. Damietta, Egypt
16. Suez Canal Transit
17. Malta
18. La Spezia, Italy
19. Tilbury, England
20. Hamburg, Germany
21. Rotterdam, Holland
22. Dunkirk, France
23. Le Havre, France
24. New York, USA

Acknowledgments

WRITING IS A LONELY TASK, BUT IT IS NOT DONE IN A VACUUM.

Every author needs a subject. In my case it was the world, and M/V CMA CGM MANET. I thank the officers and crew for their competence and companionship, especially my steward and friend, Mr. Crispin D. Apatan. Salamat (Thank you) Criss.

I was enlightened, and this book was enriched by my traveling companions, Reg and Lynne Lowe, Carl and Pancha Peterson, and Lia Van Der Lann

Somewhere in this manuscript I took responsibility for all mistakes. My burden would have been much greater had it not been for these friends who were kind enough to correct me. Jessica Feth, Iris Beaupre, Elaine Hartley, Louise Cyr, Jean Egan, and Ronald Hartley.

Both love and thanks go to my partner and dear wife Marise. Her love, encouragement, and support constitute my personal world.

Preface

Look around you. Is the world flat? Prior to 300 BC your ancestors thought it was. It was then that Aristotle revolutionized thinking with his hypothesis that the world was round. Yet eighteen centuries later, in 1492 when Columbus set sail, some of his crew still thought the world was flat and if they sailed too far they would drop off the edge of the earth. Even today, the Flat Earth Society remains a bastion of believers in the theory that we live on a flat planet.

In pursuit of knowledge, adventure, and perhaps a bit of humor, I plan to sail from America in a westerly direction. If our ship circumnavigates the earth and returns in three months, Aristotle's hypothesis is proven and the world is round. If we fail to return, it will no doubt mean that we have fallen off the edge of the earth, never to be heard from again, and the earth is indeed flat.

Along the way we will see new sights, experience new adventures, and we may even learn a few facts, especially about geography and nautical ways. We will be traveling by freighter. Unlike a luxurious cruise ship with constant entertainment and pampering, this will be a working ship where passengers are at the low end of the priority list and are responsible for their own well-being. We voyagers will be few in number, strangers at first, and responsible for our own diversions. But we will live in private quarters, have access to areas off limits on cruise ships, and dine with the officers.

Preparation for this trip began in the spring of 2003. Traveling on a regular cruise ship normally requires choosing a destination and making one phone call to a travel agent. Booking passage on a freighter is far more complicated. Travel agents are not interested in this work and shipping companies, who provide the accommodations, hesitate to get involved with individuals; therefore one must seek the services of a few specialized agents who provide this service.

The Internet has several Web sites that deal with freighter reservations and while their inventory of shorter, intercontinental trips is sufficient, their round-the-world inventory is limited to a handful of companies providing fewer then a dozen passenger- carrying freighters. Furthermore, there are usually only two or three passenger cabins available on each of these ships resulting in a rather sparse selection for the potential round-the-world traveler.

After several fruitless attempts, I contacted Captain Ranko Zunic, President of Maris Freighter Cruises, (www.freightercruisis.com), who was able to book passage for me on the *Manet*, a container ship operated by The French Line, CMA CGM. The $9,990, eighty-four-day voyage is scheduled to depart from New York City on January 9, 2004. Prior to departure I must check my passport, purchase insurance, get a visa for Australia, get a physical, and get a shot for yellow fever.

This book will be written in real time. You will read about the adventure as it unfolds. You will be there when the ship departs and you may feel queasy when it starts to roll. You will see new sights abroad and be part of everyday life on board, and if you pay attention, we may both learn a thing or two about our world. So check your passport and get your shot, it's time to cast off.

And by the way, if the thought of falling off the edge of the earth has made you hesitant about this journey; *now hear this*, the world is round, you will return, and you are more then welcome to come aboard. Care to join me?

Introduction

Times Square, crossroads of the world, is hereby designated "Official Starting Point" for our trip. Times Square, fewer then five miles from where our ship will dock, is actually a triangle, with geographical coordinates of 40°45'30"N, 073°59'09" W. We will learn all about coordinates later in the trip. For now, the question is, how did this trip mature from a daydream to a day of departure?

Before discussing the logistics of preparing for a round-the-world voyage, it would seem appropriate to explain *why* I want to circle the globe. What reason would there be to spend $10,000 and leave the comforts and security of home for three months? Adventure, thrill of travel, meet new people, are all good reasons, but they seem trivial. From past travels I know that an extended trip in unfamiliar surroundings strips away our blanket of routine, producing a stimulating experience. That is my objective. And why am I traveling alone? My dear wife Marise is a wonderful woman and we have explored together for forty-six years, but she is not a sailor. She has chosen to forgo this trip and stay on dry land in Florida. I shall miss her.

After securing the trip with a deposit in May, Marise and I spent the summer traveling in our motorhome. Six weeks of hosting at a campground in Shenandoah National Park were followed by a summer in Maine, and that was followed by six more weeks hosting during a gorgeous fall at a Vermont State Park. During that time I continued researching and planning the trip which, for me, is half the joy of doing anything new. Preparation has an inverse ratio to problems. When one goes up, the other goes down.

I also made the decision to write this book; or at least keep an extensive diary which could be converted to a book if the trip were interesting enough. For more than ten years I have kept a daily diary, and in 2002 used it as a basis for my first book, CARE TO JOIN ME?, Day by day on the Appalachian Trail. While the book has yet to make it to a best seller list, it is of great personal value to me. It not only preserved the memories of my five-month hike from Georgia to Maine, but I found that the act of recording events each day forced me to pay more attention to those events as they occurred, thereby enriching the entire experience. I regret that I did not start keeping a diary earlier in life. At seventy, what a joy it would be to read, in detail, about the escapades of my youth.

Having made the decision to write a second book, I knew there were bound to be some dull days and to keep the reader's interest, they would need to be spiced up. I resolved that those days at sea, when shipboard activities were routine and repetitious, would be converted to days at school. This book will not only be a travel adventure, but also a learning experience for my grandchildren to whom it is dedicated, and for anyone else interested in the basics of our world. This meant that I had to bone up on high school studies and gather information on other interesting subjects that would fit the storyline.

So be aware, upon completion of this book you will not only have traveled around the world, but you may also become the trivia champ of your block. For example, did you know that the world's largest passenger ship is on its maiden voyage as this is being written? The *Queen Mary 2* is 1130 feet long, as high as a twenty-one-story building, and will accommodate over 2600 passengers. A ticket on the $800 million, 150,000-ton trans-Atlantic liner will cost between $1,150 and $34,500. Now you know.

In September, during our stay in Vermont, I purchased the required traveler's insurance and secured an Australian visa, all with a few clicks on the Internet. In October, I had a cursory physical and got the required yellow fever shot. After completing the necessary paperwork, I visited Captain Ronko Zunic and his wife Maja at Maris Freighter Cruises. Captain Zunic, a former ship's Master, had the firsthand knowledge to thoroughly answer questions about our approaching trip.

By December we had settled in at the RV resort in Florida where Marise will spend the winter. On December 22 after receiving tickets and boarding information, I made travel and lodging reservations for the trip to New York. With preparation all but complete, I passed through the Christmas holiday season in a daze, always with one eye on departure day.

On the morning of Thursday, January 8, Marise and I stood on the train platform at Kissimmee, Florida awaiting the arrival of the Silver Meteor. We had been through separations like this before and while there is no easy way to say goodby, we believe however you do it, do it quickly. Lacking celestial speed, the Meteor was almost two hours late, making that difficult, but separate we did, knowing that it would be three months before we embraced again.

Twenty-four hours later I was settled in at the Hotel Pennsylvania. The Hotel Pennsylvania bills itself as "The World's Most Popular Hotel" and those of you over fifty may remember the 1940 Glenn Miller tune, Pennsylvania-6-5000. Of course their phone number is now updated with an area code but you still hear that tune when you call the hotel switchboard.

A quick call to Port Agent James Craddock brought me the disappointing news that the *Manet* was not expected to arrive until Monday, stretching an expected one-night stay into an expensive three-day weekend in New York. Normally I would relish a weekend in New York, but under the circumstances my mind was on the trip and also the weather was bitterly cold with wind chill temperatures below zero. Nevertheless, I passed the time by making a dry run to Brooklyn, where the ship was to dock, and attending, of all things, an "Adventure Travel Expo." They touted everything from cruises to the Amazon to exploration of the North Pole, but no freighter trips. On Sunday evening I got a call from Mr. Craddock advising me that the *Manet* had arrived and I could board anytime after 7:00 A.M. tomorrow.

The hour is late in this period of preparation. Alone in my hotel room I try to review all the details that got us here to make sure nothing is forgotten. But in truth it is too late for change. In truth it is time to turn and look ahead to tomorrow, to the opening chapter of this saga. I expect the remainder of this night to be restless, haunted by those fickle feelings of apprehension– what have I gotten into?, and jubilation–departure day has finally arrived! But these thoughts will only serve to keep me awake. In truth, we are committed.

Before we begin this journey, let me make one suggestion. In all honesty the maps in this book leave much to be desired. If you are seriously interested in geography, and you should be, spend a few bucks and get a good world map. Better yet, dig the globe out of your closet, dust it off, and place it by your favorite reading chair. Either one will increase the value of your trip and may even keep you from getting lost at sea.

CHAPTER ONE

Atlantic Ocean
New York ⇒ Norfolk ⇒ Savannah ⇒

Mon. Jan 12, 2004   40° 41'14" N
000 Mi. / 00000 Total Miles   074° 00'35" W

Transition is too weak a word for today's events. This morning I woke up in New York City, familiar surroundings for me. Seventy years ago I was born in Manhattan, grew up in New Jersey, and as a teenager, often roamed the streets of this fascinating city. After college this was home for several years while working on the Verrazano Narrows Bridge. Tonight I will sleep at sea, resting on a strange bed in an alien world. The events of today transcend transition, they are a major change, a giant leap. However, after walking the decks of this ship for a few days, it too will become familiar and I will again feel at home. Some of us worry about, and resist change, others seek it out and are enriched by it. Since you are still with us, you belong in the latter group. Welcome to our new neighborhood.

I write this about 8:00 P.M. as we head southbound somewhere off the coast of New Jersey. A few solitary beacons struggle through the darkness but the bright lights of the Atlantic City casinos are hidden somewhere over the horizon. This is truly a new world.

After a parting call to Marise, I left the hotel headed toward the subway, pack on my back and pulling a large suitcase behind. The F Train took me under the East River to Brooklyn faster and cheaper than any taxi during Monday morning's rush hour. From the subway it was a half-mile walk to the docks where the security guard checked my ticket and passport. Pointing toward the *Manet* he advised, "Watch the trucks out there, they could spoil your trip." Dodging trucks and forklifts, I got to the *Manet* and was spotted by a deckhand who came down and carried my fifty-pound suitcase up the gangplank. On board, an officer greeted me, asked if I carried weapons, drugs, explosives, alcohol, or tobacco, then summoned Crispin, the steward, to show me to my cabin. Minutes later the Radio Officer came in and asked to see my tickets, passport, physical, and yellow fever record. He carefully studied them and left. After years of dreaming and months of planning, I was on board!

Now what? Without a recreational director what does one do? I spent the next fifteen minutes pinching myself and then headed out to see what I could see. There are eighty-four days left in this trip for details of what I saw. Here, on day one, we will only skim the surface.

At noon I headed down to lunch and there met Carl and Pancha who had boarded just before me. They are going as far as Auckland, New Zealand and at first glance seem to be good fellow travelers.

The afternoon was filled with exploration, unpacking, and observing. Observing primarily the loading and positioning of giant containers as though they were little blocks of wood.

Just before dinner Reginald and Lynne returned on board from their one-day excursion of New York City. Right jolly English folks they appear to be, so it seems we are in luck with our traveling companions.

Halfway through dinner I felt the ship move and quickly excused myself to go watch our departure. At 6:30 it was dark, cold, spitting snow, with a raw wind out of the north—but I couldn't be happier. The next hour was one of the emotional highs of my life as worries of preparation turned into excitement of exploration. A tiny tug pulled along side and the *Manet* came alive, inching her bow away from the dock. Slipping our moorings, we entered the mouth of the Hudson River and were caught in its current flowing out through South Bay toward the Atlantic. As the lights of Manhattan faded, we passed under the Verrazano Narrows Bridge. She gave us a curtsey as a fond farewell.

Tue. Jan 13   35° 35′ 21″ N
355 Mi. / 355 Total Miles   074° 52′ 20″ W

Rule number one of freighter travel—be flexible. We are going to bypass Norfolk, Virginia which was to have been our first stop. Probably because of the two-day delay crossing the Atlantic, Norfolk will be dropped and its cargo will be off-loaded at Savannah, then transferred back to Norfolk on a smaller, feeder ship. Reg and his wife Lynne who got on at Tilbury, England, said that although the ship's speed was greatly reduced during their Atlantic crossing due to high winds and thirty-foot waves, they experienced little discomfort and, in fact, rather enjoyed the experience.

On this first full day at sea I awoke early with the moon shining through the porthole. We have already left the dreary cold of New York and reached clear skies and a warmer Gulf Stream. We are about fifty miles off the coast, not far enough to fight the Gulf Stream's northerly current, but close enough to feel its warmth.

Breakfast is served between 0730 and 0830 in the officer's dining room. Five passengers sit at one round table and a second rectangular table can seat six officers. Rather than discussing food each day, let me show you a typical menu. So far we have had wine at lunch and dinner, and I would expect that to continue.

CMA CGM MANET MENU
Jan. 13 Tuesday
<u>Breakfast</u>
FRESH MILK / CHILLED ORANGE JUICE
ASSTD. CEREALS
EGGS TO ORDER
FRIED CORN BEEF HASH
BAKED BEANS / PLUM TOMATO
FRESH BAKED BREAD
MARMALADE / JAM / BUTTER
COFFEE OR TEA
<u>Lunch</u>
SOUP: GARLIC SOUP W/CROUTON
SALAD, GREEK SALAD
M. COURSE: STIR FRY BEEF TIPS' W/VEGETABLE,
CHIPS, FRIED EGG PLANT
FRESH BAKED BREAD
DESSERT: CUSTARD WITH TOPPINGS
COFFEE OR TEA
<u>Dinner</u>
SOUP OF THE DAY
SALAD OF THE DAY
ENTREE: SPAGHETTI CARBONARA
M. COURSE: CHICKEN IN TOMATO HERB, BOILED POTATO,
BUTTERED PASTA, STEAMED RICE, BROCCOLI
ASSTD. CHEESE/COLD CUTS
FRESH BAKED BREAD
DESSERT: FRUIT CAKE W/CUSTARD
COFFEE OR TEA

Meals are served by Crispin or Criss as he prefers, the steward I mentioned earlier. Criss is Filipino, as are most of the crew members below officer level. This morning as he cleaned my room he gave a snapshot of his life. He has a twelve-year-old son and an eight-year-old daughter. He works on the ship for nine months, seven days a week, then takes three months vacation which is roughly equivalent to three trips around and one off per year. Each day he reports to the galley at 0600 and is on duty until 2000 but that includes several long breaks. His English is sufficient for the job and will doubtless improve as he works with English-speaking passengers. His pay and tips must be good compared to wages in the Philippines to justify his sacrifice of separation. Passengers are expected to tip the steward between $3-5 per day, per person, but no other crew member is normally tipped.

Criss, our Steward

You may have noticed that I used the twenty-four-hour clock which is standard on board. To use the twenty-four-hour clock simply add 12 to any time after the noon hour. I know that most of you know what the twenty-four-hour clock is and you don't need my explanation, but please remember, this book is also meant for Kaitlin, my five-year-old granddaughter. Throughout the book I might explain a number of things just for her. I am not patronizing you.

Wed, Jan 14   32° 07′ 12″N
432Mi. / 787 Total Miles   081° 08′ 02″W

If there is a warm breeze and the streets are lined with moss-covered oak trees, we must be in Savannah, Georgia, one of the gems of the South. At 0530 I was awakened when the engine's vibration, all but forgotten at sea, slowed to a crawl. This constant throb only becomes noticeable when it changes. In the darkness I walked out on deck and there, about twenty miles away, were the lights of a refinery marking the entrance to Savannah River and the City of Savannah five miles upstream, our first land sighting since leaving New York. The city was still asleep as we crept past at 0700, but by 0900 when we finally docked five miles upstream, the port was alive and ready to welcome our cargo.

Not knowing the procedure for leaving the ship, I checked with Danny, the radio officer, who seems to be our liaison. He advised that we must wait for the port agent before anything happens. An hour later he gave us our passports and a reboarding slip and told us to be back on board by 2200. Moments later Reg, Lynne, and I started off, snaking our way through mountains of containers, looking for the yard gate. Five minutes later, a police officer picked us up, took us to the gate, and had Security call a taxi. Southern hospitality still lives. Reg and Lynne got out in town and I continued on with Pat, our driver, to find a Wal-Mart for some odds and ends. Pat had been robbed the week before, and as she vividly described how the robber had held a gun to her head, I wished that she would keep her hands on the wheel.

About noon I caught a bus back to town after unsuccessfully trying to contact Marise several times by phone. Savannah is a lovely town, laid out in small squares with many of them set aside for parks filled with fountains and ancient oaks, a great town for walking. The waterfront has been restored to a "Riverwalk" lined with the usual tourist shops and a statue of Florence Martus. The story goes that Florence fell in love with a sailor who went to sea with a promise to return to marry her. For forty-four years she waved a towel at every passing ship hoping for a sign of his return. Only a bronze statue marks her spot now but I will wave back as we pass by tonight.

The Waving Girl

Marise and I have visited Savannah several times, always enjoying it, especially in the spring when the azaleas are in bloom. Finally I was able to get through on her cell phone and we each relayed our news. I told her the details of our trip so far and all was well on her end. She seems to be quite comfortable and confident in her new surroundings, which makes my trip more pleasurable.

I was able to catch a bus back to within a mile of the port and had no trouble getting back in after checking through Security again.

At dinner tonight I mentioned that this ship is already starting to feel like home, becoming a welcome sight after a day in town. Still, all is not perfect. They blocked the forward view from my porthole today, and Danny told me tonight that I must have a floppy disk in order to send e-mail through the ships satellite system. Maybe I can get an external floppy in Panama. However, far more serious, Pancha found out that her eighty-six-year-old mother is in the hospital. Terrible timing for Pancha with the ship now leaving the U.S. for good.

Thu, Jan 15   30° 06′ 09″N
177 Mi. / 964 Total Miles   079° 18′ 06″W

I had good intentions of blowing a kiss to The Waving Girl as we departed Savannah but at midnight they were still loading containers leaving me no choice but to turn in. As we slept, the *Manet* slipped out of port at 0200. I briefly woke around 0300 as the thump of the engine and roll of ocean swells signaled our return to sea.

On this fourth day at sea a semblance of routine has set in. Surprising how quickly we adapt to pleasure. The initial excitement has faded and we are now reasonably familiar with our surroundings. You might say we feel at home. After breakfast we each go our separate ways and I found myself on the bridge deck. Our weather has turned warm and humid, not uncomfortable yet, but pleasant. Yesterday's paper said that it was expected to drop to zero degrees in New York last night. It seems so far away in distance and climate.

After some small talk with the officer on watch I went outside, and for the first time the vastness of these boundless seas hit me. From this vantage point we can turn 360 degrees and see nothing but a blue grandness speckled with white foam and an occasional breaking wave. The setting would mesmerize even the most hardened soul, wakening thoughts of heaven on earth. From our height of over eighty feet the curvature of the horizon left no doubt that the world truly is round.

However, I have a book to write and cannot lollygag around all day watching waves. It is too early in the trip to speak of a pattern but around 0900 I have been returning to my cabin, getting a cup of coffee, and reviewing what was written the night before. At 1000 I get the daily coordinates of our position with a basic GPS unit and plot where we are and how far we have traveled in the past twenty-four hours.

Before departure I had programed the coordinates of the RV resort where Marise is staying into this gadget and by pushing a few buttons, I noted that for the first time, the distance between our locations was increasing. Heading south from New York, I had been getting closer to Marise in Florida each day, as close as one hundred-forty-one miles at one point. Now I was drawing away from her and it left a melancholy feeling. I'm sure I will miss her more as time and distance grows.

Before I knew it, lunch was being served and Reg was telling us that he had heard that the ship took on one thousand tons of fuel at Savannah which will get us to Panama. Five thousand tons, yes, that's right, tons, are needed to propel this ship around the world. I have no idea what this fuel costs, but it is the heavy sludge that is left in the refining process after gasoline and lighter oils are taken off. It is called bunker fuel and is so thick that it must be heated before it will flow.

Reg, short for Reginald, got on at Tilbury, England with his wife, Lynne. He is a large well-built man in his late fifties, bald as a billiard. He has a very quick wit and also a very quick tongue which sometimes I find difficult to understand because he speaks "English English," if you know what I mean. Lynne, who always has a wonderful smile, seems like the perfect English mother. She is the quiet partner, probably from living with Reg for many years. Anyway, Reg was full of information today. At dinner he told us that while up at the bow he had seen flying fish and a huge turtle. Imagine, one hundred miles offshore and there's a turtle flapping along fifty feet from the ship.

Flying fish are found worldwide in warm waters. In this area they are slightly bigger then your hand and are gray in color. They emerge from the water like a shot with wings (pectoral fins) outstretched, gliding just above the surface. Some species are said to be able to travel up to six-hundred feet and attain a height of thirty feet. Their flight is a means of escaping predators—like the bow of our ship.

Enough gossip for the day. Tonight we are in international waters headed away from the good old U.S. of A. Many more characters, chronicles, and countries lay over the horizon so don't jump ship yet.

Fri, Jan 16   22° 56' 09"N
572 Mi. / 1546 Total Miles   074° 38' 59"W

Uniform of the day is a tee shirt and shorts. Put away those sweaters and gloves till we cross the North Atlantic in April. At 1700 we were passing through the fifty-mile wide channel between Cuba and Haiti, leaving the Atlantic Ocean and entering the Caribbean Sea. Thunderstorms were pelting the Cubans as we passed by. Guantanamo Bay, the U.S. Navel Station is about fifty miles away on the far side of the island. The sea has turned an iridescent blue reflecting a shallower depth and light-colored bottom, every sailors dream.

Island of Cuba

Carl and Pancha will be coming back here next year on their own private yacht. An interesting couple, they appear to be well bred, well read, and well heeled. They own a forty-four-foot yacht and both seem to have the necessary experience to make good use of it. Each morning Carl goes to the bridge before breakfast to gather information about our past, present, and future location. He then relays it to us at the breakfast table in a language that I, as a landlubber, can understand. Pancha has been kind enough to read my book, *CARE TO JOIN ME?* Her review shall remain confidential, but we continue to sit side by side at the dining table.

Conversation at the dining table is both interesting and lively at times. Did you know that the proper title for the senior officer of a ship this size is Master? You may address them as Captain, but Master differentiates them from rowboat captains. "Master" may seem a bit excessive, but these chaps do carry a lot of responsibility with a hundred-million-dollar ship and fifty-million dollars of cargo. Speaking of cargo, occasionally one or more of these containers will fall off a ship in bad weather which could spoil the Master's day. Along with the loss of cargo, the container will float at the surface or just below it as long as the air inside is sufficient to buoy it.

We are now in the Caribbean, tropical paradise and start of Chapter Two of this adventure. Refresh your pinacolada and read on.

Caribbean Sea
⇒ Manzanillo ⇒ Panama Canal ⇒

Sat, Jan 17   14° 56′ 20″N
570 Mi. / 2116 Total Miles   076° 50′ 00″W

Let's face it, there are going to be days on this trip when nothing happens. Yesterday we entered the Caribbean Sea, today we sailed across it. The water was calm and blue, the sky was dotted with puffy clouds, and the Master turned on the ships air-conditioning. You know things are slow when the A/C is big news. We followed a straight course to Panama, saw three ships, saw no land, and nothing happened.

What do you write about on a day like today? My day was not as idyllic as our surroundings might suggest. That is the subject.

The words in Chapter One did not float down from heaven and organize themselves into coherent sentences. And they did not flow from my pen with effortless ease. No, they had to be pulled out one by one, shaped into a meaningful thought, then forced into the computer. I had completed that task, printed out a draft of Chapter One, and arranged with Pancha to read it. Then I found that an entire page had been deleted, disappeared, vanished into vapor. That may sound inconsequential to the reader, but it is traumatic to the writer.

Writing is difficult, especially when you self publish as I do. When this masterpiece is finished, a CD with the complete layout, text, pictures, cover, misspelled words, and mistakes will be sent to the publisher. The publisher will put that CD into his computer and print all those mistakes under the name of Bob Hartley. There is no editor, no reviewer, no proofreader. No one checks anything. You stand there completely exposed, responsible for the fabulous phrases and your grammatical gaffes. Like a nudist showing all his wonders and warts, you, as a writer, expose yourself to the world.

I wouldn't have it any other way. This is my creation; if you derive even the slightest pleasure from it, or if it sparks one child to think, I have done my job, warts and all. Writers don't write for themselves.

The missing page was rewritten from memory, Pancha was helpful and kind in her review, and we are one day closer to Panama.

Sun, Jan 18   09° 21′ 24″N
437 Mi. / 2553 Total Miles   079° 52′ 57″W

Tonight we are anchored five miles off the coast of Panama, awaiting our turn to enter the Panama Canal tomorrow morning. For a ship this size, a reservation for the Canal transit must be made a month in advance. It will be a highlight of our trip.

Today began at 0300 when the thump, thump, thump of the engine slowed to a crawl. The roll of the sea and rhythm of the engine act like a sedative, but they become an alarm clock when they suddenly stop. As I left the air-conditioned cabin and walked out on deck, I was struck with the heavy, humid, smell of a tropical rain forest. Lights in the distance identified the port city of Manzanillo, Panama, and the thought occurred that from here, South America is only two hundred miles away. I've never been there but it has a succulent smell.

Three hours later we were tied up at port and at breakfast we learned the second rule of freighter travel–be flexible. This was not to be a day in town as expected. Scheduling was tight and as soon as the transfer of cargo was complete, we would be leaving dockside to go to our present anchored position. I assume that ships pay large fees for the use of wharf space. That is why we are parked out here in the bay for free. We were given the option to go into town but then we would have to pay three hundred dollars to hire a boat taxi to get us out to the anchored *Manet*. I'm sorry, the best I can do is offer a picture of Manzanillo. It is not a three- hundred-dollar town.

Manzanillo, Panama

Our original itinerary also included Panama City on the Pacific side of Panama, but that port was dropped last summer, so when we clear the canal, it's straight to Tahiti. This means that I won't get an external floppy disk in Panama City, nor will I make a phone call to Marise. Realizing this, Pancha asked if I would care to send an e-mail through their computer and floppy, which I did. I hope Marise gets it; Tahiti is ten days away.

After dinner I took a walk around the deck and got the feeling that I was on the Strip at Las Vegas. Normally at night we run with minimum outside lighting because it interferes with nighttime vision.

The other night a crew member knocked at the door and asked me to close my curtains because the light from my porthole was reflecting off the containers and hindering the helmsman's vision. Tonight is just the opposite. Every ship, and there are at least twenty-five out there, is lit up like a Christmas tree, and each casts its shimmer across the water. This, of course, is because we are all anchored out here near a shipping channel and being visible is smart.

Mon, Jan 19   09° 20′ 57′ N
3Mi. / 2556 Total Miles   079° 55′ 57′ W

Let's go! Feet on the floor and out the door. This is going to be a big day so let's wipe the cobwebs from our eyes, we are going to make our first trip through the Panama Canal. It's 0645, the morning sun is still hiding behind that cloud bank, but activity will soon start. Before breakfast let's review the Canal's history and see how it works.

The Panama Canal was built by the U.S. Government between 1904 and 1914 at a cost of $350 million. It connects the Atlantic and Pacific Oceans and is fifty miles long including the approach channels at each end. To get over the mountains in Panama, a ship must be raised a total of eighty-five feet, then lowered back down. This is done by going through "locks," and to know how locks work, all you have to remember is that water runs downhill.

A lock is like a giant bathtub, large enough to hold our ship and having doors at each end. To simplify things, let's say that the Atlantic Ocean (sea level)is at one end of our bathtub and Gatún Lake is at the other. Gatún Lake is twenty-six miles long and right in the middle of Panama. It is eighty-five feet above sea level and one of the largest artificially created lakes in the world. Without Gatún Lake, there would be no canal. First, we open the Atlantic Ocean door to our bathtub and our ship floats in. Then we close that door and open the valve on a pipe which runs from Gatún Lake into our bathtub. Because Gatún Lake is at eighty-five feet, water flows downhill into our bathtub and raises our ship eighty-five feet. Now we open the door to Gatún Lake and float across it. On the Pacific side we have another bathtub filled with Gatún Lake water. We open the Gatún Lake door, float our ship in, and close that door. Now we open a valve on a pipe to the Pacific Ocean. Once again water runs downhill and our ship is lowered back to sea level. After opening the Pacific Ocean door we float out into the Pacific.

Of course it's not that simple. Actually there are three locks at each end of Gatún Lake and they each raise or lower a ship one third of the eighty-five feet. And we don't just float in; there are tugs, mules, pilots, and others that get us through the Canal. Let's go watch.

0730   First we'll have breakfast. It's going to be a long day.
0840   The *Manet* weighs anchor and begins a slow move toward Limon Bay.
0910   We pass the breakwater.
0940   A boat delivers the pilot who will command the ship as it passes through the Canal.

1000   I take my daily latitude and longitude reading.
1025   Two tugs come alongside
1035   Limon Bay begins to narrow. The channel is busy with work boats, tugs, security, etc.

1040   We pick up eighteen men who will handle the lines and perform other canal related duties as we pass through.

1100   The tugs have guided us to a position just outside the first set of locks and we are being secured to "mules" which are small electric locomotives that run on tracks beside the locks. I always thought that the mules pulled the ship through the locks. Wrong. They just keep it centered in the lock with ropes so that it doesn't rub the sides.

1107   We can see the massive seven-foot-thick gates to lock number one in front of us starting to open.

1110   The pilot orders our ship dead-slow ahead and eight mules, two at each corner, follow along with their ropes keeping us centered. Each lock is 1000' long and 110' wide. Our ship is 642' long and 99' wide so we have about five feet of clearance on each side.

1120   The gates to the Atlantic close behind us and water starts to fill
       our lock thru pipes at the bottom.

1125   It is almost imperceptible, but very slowly the water begins to
       lift our thirty-thousand-ton ship with all its cargo.

1140   We are now almost thirty feet higher than the ship beside us.
       The canal has side by side locks throughout resembling a two-
       lane shipping highway.

1150   The gates between locks one and two are now open and the
       mules steady us as we move into lock two.

1220   We are now in lock three, eighty-five feet above sea level. The
       canal headquarters is here with a viewing platform allowing
       those on land to see just a little bit of what we are fortunate
       enough to experience in entirety. Gatún Lake is spread out
       before us, dotted with a cruise ship and several freighters
       waiting their turn to take the lock stairway down to the
       Atlantic.

1300 Gatún Lake lies within the Canal Zone. There are no homes, no condos, and no industries along the shores. Only a few official buildings spotted here and there amongst the trees. It is a large, peaceful lake which belies the fact that each year more than fifteen thousand ships of every size carry the world's cargo across its waters. We will soon be approaching Gaillard Cut, one of the most difficult sections to build because of unstable earth here at the Continental Divide.

1600 For the past three hours we have been sailing at eighty-five feet through Gatún Lake. Now we are approaching the Miraflores Locks where we will reverse this morning's procedure and step down through three locks back to sea level and the Pacific Ocean. Throughout the day we have seen signs of proper maintenance and progress. This canal, which was built by the United States, is now owned and maintained by the country of Panama.

1800   On the trip back down to the Pacific, after passing through the upper gate, we cross two-mile-wide Miraflores Lake. That is where we are now, and we are about to eat dinner. We missed lunch and I don't know about you, but I'm starved.

1905   We are entering the middle lock on our way down. It is dark now and we spot a beautiful cargo of yachts on the ship beside us which is going up the stairway toward the Atlantic. Carl, who knows his boats, says they were probably made in New Zealand.

1940   As the gates of the last lock open we can smell the Pacific. Eleven hours after leaving the Atlantic, we are dipping our keel into the Pacific. Amazing! Without the Panama Canal early passages from New York to San Francisco took months and were threatened by terrible weather when they rounded Cape Horn at the tip of South America. Even today, large ships which cannot fit through the locks take weeks to transit between these oceans, and we did it in under half a day!

2000   One more sight to behold. As we leave the Panama Canal and head out into the Pacific Ocean, we pass under the Bridge of the Americas, the only bridge connecting North and South America.

CHAPTER THREE

Pacific Ocean

⇒ Papeete ⇒ Auckland ⇒

Tue, Jan 20	05° 58' 44"N
316 Mi. / 2872 Total Miles	083° 02' 06"W

Today feels like the day after Super Bowl Sunday. The big event has come and gone, everyone knows the outcome, it is time to return to work. Our Super Bowl was the Panama Canal; we now have seen it and it's time to move on.

This morning's geographical coordinates placed us in the South Pacific, about two hundred miles off the coast of Ecuador. Our heading is, and will remain, approximately 250 degrees (west-southwest) for the next eight days until we reach Papeete, Tahiti. This seems like a good time to introduce SCHOOL DAYS. School Days consists of about a dozen articles, a page or so in length, that are meant to interest, entertain, and enlighten. From time to time I shall slip one in to keep us awake. Please don't let the title scare you off. They are meant for any age and all levels of intelligence, and there are no exams; give them a try.

Nautical Terms

Amidship	Center of the ship
Astern	Behind the ship
Beam	The widest part of the ship
Bollard	Post on pier for mooring ships lines
Bow	Front of the ship
Break bulk	Mixed freight
Bridge	Control center of the ship
Bulk carrier	Carries loose solids: wheat, ore, timber, etc.
Bulkhead	Vertical partition or wall
Car carrier	Designed for transporting vehicles only
Container ship	Designed for transporting containers only
Draft	Depth of ship below water
Fathom	Measure of water depth equal to six feet
Galley	Ship's kitchen
Head	Ship's bathroom
Helmsmen	One who steers the ship

Knot	Measure of speed equal to 1.15 statute mi/hr
Latitude	See Pg. 22
Lee	Area sheltered from the wind
Longitude	See Pg. 22
Master	Ship's captain
Mayday	Distress call with possible loss of life or ship
Nautical mile	6,080 feet or 1 minute of latitude
Pan Pan	Distress call with unlikely loss of life or ship
Plimsoll line	Mark on hull showing max. legal load limit
Poop Deck	Raised deck at the stern of a ship
Port	Left side of ship
Porthole	Window
Quay	Dock parallel to shore for berthing ship
Ro-Ro	Roll on- Roll off (cargo is anything on wheels)
Rudder	Steers the ship
Running lights	Required when ship is underway in darkness
Screw	Ships propeller
Starboard	Right side of ship
Statute mile	5280 feet
Stern	Rear of ship
TEU	Twenty-foot Equivalent Units (containers)
Tanker	Carries liquid, usually oil
Tender	Small boat / Ship that tips easily
Tramp	Bulk carrier ships
Watch	Period of responsibility for the ship
Wharf	Dock structure
Windward	Into the wind

Wed, Jan 21   03° 19' 40" N
572 Mi. / 3444 Total Miles   090° 53' 20" W

Yesterday, our bow broke the surface of a calm and placid sea. It appeared that we were sailing on a glass mirror shattered only by our wake which stretched for miles behind us. A cloudless sky brought the sun down at full strength making deck chairs uncomfortable.

Today, a light drizzle makes it necessary to find a sheltered spot for deck chairs and a breeze blows out of the north stirring the ocean surface enough to quickly swallow our wake, erasing our trail.

At 1100 we passed approximately one hundred and eighty miles north of the Galapagos Islands. The Galapagos group is noted for its animal life, which includes numerous species found only in the archipelago. During the 17th and 18th centuries, pirates used the islands as a rendezvous point, but in 1835 the naturalist, Charles Darwin, traveling aboard the HMS *Beagle,* spent six weeks studying its animal life and brought a different kind of notoriety to the islands.

His observations formed the basis for his 1859 work, *On the Origin of Species.* Prior to Darwin, most geologists adhered to the so-called catastrophist theory which theorized that our world is periodically subjected to catastrophes and after each, a new set of animal and plant life has developed. That is how they accounted for the fossils of animals that no longer existed. Darwin's theory of evolution postulated that in each species the stronger members were the survivors, and consequently their characteristics tended to be handed down to future generations. Therefore, each generation will improve ever so slightly and this gradual and continuous process is the source of change or, as he termed it, evolution of the species.

There were immediate outcries from religious opponents. The idea that life had evolved from a natural process denied God and the special creation of mankind, putting humans at the same level as animals. The controversy exists to this day. Evolution vs. Creation.

On a less scholarly note, Reg and Lynne reported seeing a school of dolphins off the bow this morning. At dinner the five of us could not agree as to whether they should be referred to as a school of dolphins or a pod of dolphins so I dutifully researched definitions. A school is a large group of marine animals and a pod is a small group of marine animals. You can define large and small, but they were a lovely sight. They also saw shearwaters, a large bird that would glide for long distances just above the bow, making use of the air pressure wave created by the mass of our ship pushing along at twenty-four miles per hour. Shearwaters spend their entire life wandering at sea unless actually nesting.

On a still lighter note, we set our clocks back tonight giving us one more hour of sleep. We will look at the subject of time zones at a future time. Good night.

WELCOME

Welcome to my cabin. We have been on board the *Manet* for ten days and it is time to take a closer look at our neighborhood. As time permits we will visit the bridge, take a stroll around the deck, check out the "gym," or see what the cook has for us in the galley. For today, come in, make yourself comfortable, and I'll show you around.

Our cabin is designated as the "Spare Officer" quarters. It is ten feet wide by eighteen feet long. As you can see, it has a bed, desk, two chairs, a leather sofa, and coffee table. By some standards it might be considered stark. There are no wall decorations except the map which I put up. There are no rugs on the tile floor and the Chinese who built this ship, must have good backs because the mattress is firm-firm. It also has a small refrigerator behind the camera which I haven't used. Lighting is more than adequate with overhead, table, and bed lamps. Also available is music from the ship's radio ranging from Beatles to Beethoven, and a telephone. I like it.

With the bath and closet, I have almost as much room as our motorhome in which Marise and I live together the year around.

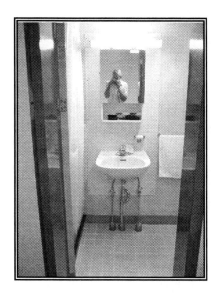 

The bath has a good size shower to the left, and a toilet to the right. The closet, just to the right of the entry door, is adequate for a Spare Officer like me. Additional storage drawers are located under the sofa and bed.

Carl and Pancha, and Reg and Lynne live in the Owner's Cabin and "Supercargo Suite" respectively. At dinner last night, they claimed with a straight face that their rooms were no better than mine, but you and I know that cabin names say it all. Actually I think the main difference is that the Owner has twin beds and Supercargo has full size. Incidently, Carl believes that Supercargo would be for someone who leased all or part of the ship.

Each morning Criss comes in and cleans the room and once a week the towels and linens are changed. Just across the hall is a free washer and dryer and two doors down there is a large conference room used primarily by the passengers for coffee and TV watching. The first officer has the room next to mine, and at the far end of the hall are quarters for the second engineer.

So now you have seen Home-Sweet-Home for the next few months. It may not be a big home, but our backyard has the world's largest swimming pool.

Fri, Jan 23   02° 23′ 56″S
563 Mi. / 4777 Total Miles   107° 48′ 14″W

There were no flags, no signs, no fences, but yesterday at 1319 we crossed the equator.

Take a close look at the above photographs. They show the ship's Global Positioning System (GPS) four seconds apart, as shown by the time in the lower right. The important figure is circled at the upper left. In the first picture the N puts us in the Northern Hemisphere; four seconds later we had moved to the Southern Hemisphere signified by the S.

I have crossed the equator before by plane, but never by ship. On a ship you can actually watch it happen. As you watch, the seconds of North Latitude decrease to zero, the N changes to S, and the seconds begin to increase again as we continue our trip south.

The clock at the lower right reads 20:19:49 which is Coordinated Universal Time (UTC). UTC is the time at the prime meridian which passes through Greenwich, England. We are in a time zone seven hours behind UTC therefore our clock read 1319. We will learn more about time zones later but today is the perfect day to take a look at Latitude and Longitude.

Latitude and Longitude

By now you have no doubt figured out what these daily headings are all about but if not, let's review our latitude and longitude. I say *our* latitude and longitude because everyone has one and only one and it is theirs and only theirs. Your latitude and longitude are simply your location on the face of this planet and as such, it is like your shadow; it is always with you and always changing as you move.

The concept of latitude and longitude was developed five hundred years ago when Portuguese map makers devised a system so their ships could safely navigate and chart all those new oceans they were discovering. They decided to place a grid over the face of the earth with all the horizontal lines (latitudes) parallel to the equator, and all the vertical lines (longitudes) going through the north and south poles. The easiest way to remember the difference between the two is: for latitude lines, picture a ladder from the south to the north poles with each rung being a latitude line. For longitude lines, picture a peeled orange with the segment lines running up and down called longitude lines. Get that; ladder for latitude and orange for longitude, or whatever works for you.

Now of course these lines have numbers or values; that's what makes them useful for locating your position on the earth. Latitude lines start at −90 at the south pole decreasing to 0 as you climb to the equator and then increasing to +90 when you reach the north pole. Longitude lines start at 0 at Greenwich, England. If you go west from there, the values increase to +180 halfway around the world. If you go east from there, the values decrease to −180 halfway around the world. In both directions, halfway around the world just happens to be the International Date Line, running north-south in the western Pacific Ocean.

You may have noticed that if we go around the equator passing the lines of longitude, also called meridians, we go from −180 to +180 or 360 degrees. Also, if we go from the south pole at −90 to the north pole at +90 on the lines of latitude, also called parallels, and then go back to the south pole, we have again gone 360 degrees. Both of these bands, around the equator and around the poles, have 360 degrees, the number of degrees in a circle, so I guess the world is round.

Getting back to our daily headings, our latitude was decreasing each day as we moved south toward the equator. Now that we have crossed the equator it will slowly increase. Note that today we are at 02° 23′ 56″S. Our longitude is increasing positively each day as we head west toward the International Date Line.

One final note. Both latitude and longitude are measured in degrees, minutes, and seconds (00° 00′ 00″N). Quiz: Go to the map at the front of this book and pick out the latitude and longitude lines.

One final, final note. I was surprised at how little attention the crew paid to our crossing of the equator. Lynne, Reg, and I were on the bridge intently watching the GPS screen as the seconds of latitude decreased. Had we a bottle of champagne, we would have popped the cork. The officer on watch paid no attention whatsoever nor did any other crew member to my knowledge. For these chaps, crossing the equator is analogous to a fly walking on the ceiling. It is unusual and interesting to the infrequent observer but natural and boring to the fly.

Sat, Jan 24   05° 15' 42"S
618 Mi. / 5395 Total Miles   116° 16' 32"W

This morning I went up to the roof of the bridge. It is eighty-five feet above water, as high as one would normally go on this ship except for maintenance of the antennas, and a wonderful spot to sunbathe and/or ruminate. When you look out from that vantage point, it is at least twenty miles before the earth's curvature swallows the ocean and you see nothing but dancing waves speckled with froth. We are completely alone, just a dot on this vast planet that we live on.

Look at the map. If we draw a circle around this ship two thousand miles in every direction, it  would only contain the ship, a few small islands, most of them uninhabited, and ocean, ocean, ocean. I'm sure that there are other ships out there somewhere in our circle, but since leaving Panama, Lynne has been the only one to spot what appeared to be a small private boat about five miles off.

That raises some interesting questions. What if someone on board becomes seriously ill or one of the deckhands had an accident? We are far out of range for a helicopter rescue. What if we had engine problems? A ship without power is vulnerable, especially to weather. What if there is an emergency back home? What if we struck a submerged obstacle? What if?

The fourth "what if" is rather far-fetched and too hypothetical to bother with. The third "what if" would be handled with communication via satellite until we reached Tahiti and then a flight home if necessary. The second "what if" is entirely possible. Ships become disabled every day and the *Manet* has been running at full sea speed, twenty-four hours a day for five days. Incidently, full sea speed on this ship is 88 RPM. That's what accounts for the thump, thump, thump that lolls us to sleep.

Thus far we have not had the privilege of visiting the engine room, but on another ship where I was granted that favor, I was amazed first at the massive size of the pistons and second at the facilities available to maintain and repair them. My guess is that our chief engineer could handle just about anything short of an overhaul right here at sea. As a final resort, there are ocean going tugs that could tow us to a repair port.

As for the first "what if," freighters do not carry doctors. Maritime Law states that any ship carrying more than twelve passengers must have a doctor on board, therefore freighters limit the size of their passenger list to twelve or fewer. But they still carry a crew that is subject to illness and accident. On the first deck of the *Manet* is a door labeled SHIP'S HOSPITAL. Again we have not seen it, but it must be equipped with adequate medical provisions to handle emergencies and it would be logical to assume that one or more of the officers has sufficient training to administer treatment backed by procedure manuals and radio consultation, if needed. So we have analyzed our possible problems and adequately planned for them should they arise.

"What if's" are a necessary part of everyday life, and we ignore them at our peril. However, once we provide for them to the best of our ability, we should set them aside and give equal energy and attention to "Why not."

Sun, Jan 25   08° 01′ 36″S
498 Mi. / 5993 Total Miles   124° 29′ 48″W

"So", you might ask, "how's life after two weeks at sea?"

To your inquiry, I would answer, "Fine, thank you," and go on to elaborate outside of quotation marks.

Four topics come to mind: two weeks, six thousand miles, acquaintance with our new surroundings, and new friends.

The days seem to fly by even though several of them have been twenty-five hour days. Tonight we set our clocks back one hour for the fourth time. Fortunately I brought one timepiece that I do not change; it is still set on Eastern Standard Time and I use that to envision what Marise is doing. As I write this, it is 7:16PM here and 11:16PM where she is. Good night, My Dear.

Six-thousand miles means nothing here. It is impossible to gauge distance at sea. Occasionally the water color changes but that is due more to cloud cover, time of day, and wind conditions. Without signposts or land sightings, which we have had none of since Panama, to guess our position we rely more on the presence of birds and location of the sun. Of course, there are always the GPS unit plus the bridge with its reams of maps if we want to get specific about location.

Our surroundings are much as expected. Over the past several years I have read everything about freighter travel that I could get my hands on so there were no major surprises. You have visited my cabin and in the future we will tour as much of the ship as permitted. We have full access to the bridge unless there is a pilot on board. At some point we may get a tour of the engine room, but I doubt we will ever see the huge cargo holds unless they have the hatch covers removed in port.

Incidently, rumor has it that the present Master of this ship will be leaving when we get to Australia. As in any organization, the person at the top sets the tone and spirit of the entire operation.

As to the fourth topic, because of the small number of passengers, a freighter traveler is always apprehensive about his fellow passengers. I have indeed been fortunate. At a minimum, the five of us spend three hours each day together at the dining table. Often because of interesting conversation, it would be more, but we don't want to inconvenience the steward.

All four of my companions are extremely well traveled and well versed in topics of the world. Tonight our conversation ranged from the British Parliament to Home Coming Queens with a dozen other subjects thrown in. Fortunately for me, no one seems to be a

Reg   Lynne   Me   Pancha   Carl

great fan of spectator sports. My knowledge of baseball and football is nil. Naturally a common topic is travel and here, although I have traveled all my life, I can barely hold my own. As Pancha ticked off the seven countries she had lived in as a child, she explained that her father was in the foreign service. Carl has traveled extensively on business as a financial expert. It is difficult to pick a place that Lynne and Reg are not familiar with. They live in England and have visited Italy twenty-seven times!

Unfortunately Carl and Pancha will be leaving when we get to Auckland in eight days. There they will rent a car and experience the wondrous sights of New Zealand before flying back to the States. We shall miss them. Rumor also has it that we will be joined by a single female at Sydney so our little group will change, but change is one of the reasons for travel.

In answer to your original question, except for the separation from Marise, I love it.

Mon, Jan 26   10° 27′ 12″S
565 Mi. / 6558 Total Miles   131° 18′ 30″W

First the facts, then the fantasy.

We are approaching an area of the world often dreamed of but seldom visited. French Polynesia covers some two million square miles of the South Pacific and is dotted with thousands of tiny islands and atolls. Names like Cook Island, Bora- Bora, Samoa, and Tahiti, which is our next stop, come to mind. Vast in area, but small in land size, all of these islands gathered together cover no more than two thousand square miles. Friendly and hospitable, the people of the South Pacific originally came from Asia to Indonesia and then used their renowned navigational skills and canoes to populate the archipelago.

A lush tropical paradise, this Territory of the French Republic has its capitol on Tahiti, the largest island, with a population of one-hundred-fifty thousand. Papeete (pronounced Pah-pay-ay-tay) is the major city on Tahiti and it is there that we will dock.

Luckily for us, Papeete is within walking distance of its commercial docks and again fortunately for us, this port has not been modernized and does not have the overhead cranes that we saw at New York and Savannah. In Papeete we will see the ship's three cranes in action for the first time. Because they are less efficient than land cranes, we will have a longer stay in port.

And now the fantasy. The following story is true, although Hollywood popularized it in the 1961 movie, *Mutiny on the Bounty* staring Marlon Brando. In 1788, Captain William Bligh sailed to Tahiti in search of breadfruit, a plant which he had seen on a previous trip with Captain James Cook. Breadfruit was sought as a cheap and nourishing food, but Bligh had to wait five months for the plants to mature. During that time his crew enjoyed the hospitality of the friendly natives and came to despise the harsh punishments metered out by Bligh. Two weeks after they left port, led by Lieutenant Fletcher Christian, part of the crew mutinied, casting Bligh adrift in a small boat with other non-mutineers.

Bligh managed to sail thirty-six-hundred miles to the Dutch Indies where he was rescued. The mutineers returned to Tahiti, gathered supplies, and set sail for the island of Pitcairn where they burned their ship and were not heard from again for eighteen years. When finally discovered by the English Navy, they had set up such a model community that the mutineers were not prosecuted. Today, some fifty of the direct descendants of Christian and the other mutineers still live an isolated life on Pitcairn Island.

The other popularization of this tropical paradise was the 1949 Broadway hit, *South Pacific*. This Rogers and Hammerstein production is regarded as one of the finest musicals ever written and won a Pulitzer Prize in 1950. Please forgive my reminiscing about watching that show from the orchestra pit, while my father played the violin and Mary Martin sang *Some Enchanted Evening*.

Tue, Jan 27   12° 58′ 07″S
502 Mi. / 7060 Total Miles   139° 20′ 35″W

We are scheduled to dock at Papeete, Tahiti at 1300 tomorrow, so today may be the right time to catch up on little items that I haven't covered during our crossing from Panama.

Item: The weather has been magnificent. Each morning my first duty is to step outside, take a deep breath of warm tropical air, sweep my eyes across the endless sea, and give thanks for being alive. We have had a few sprinkles but most days see temperatures in the low eighties, light winds, and scattered clouds. Influenced by the water to a great degree, our day and night temperatures vary only slightly, but at midday it becomes uncomfortable out in the direct sun. Reg and Lynne, who are avid sun worshipers, have had to retreat to the shade. They found a spot on the roof of the bridge, referred to as the "monkey deck," where the ship's stack casts a broad shadow. Their view surpasses that of the finest penthouse. Uniform of the day has been short-sleeve shirts and shorts.

Item: Since day one, dress has been casual. Upscale if you like, but keep it simple. Everyone on board wears shorts except where uniform requires long pants or coveralls. The officers wear white shirts with the appropriate epaulets and a casual pair of shorts while on duty or dining. One item I did not bring and plan to buy in Papeete, is a pair of sandals. Of course as we move to cooler climates, dress will change but the style will remain casual.

Item: Breakfast hour has been changed from 0730 to 0700. No one knows why.

Item: This ship is immaculate. It was launched on May 2, 2001 and to the credit of officers and crew, it looks as it did on that first day. At 0530 this morning Criss was cleaning the hallway floor which you can already eat off. Every day when I take my walk to the bow, some new surface is being scraped or painted by a crew member which brings to mind another thought: They never stop. Yesterday, Sunday, was a work day like all the others. If you're into walking down on the cargo deck you will return with a slight film of oil on your hands which is easily washed off. This comes from the gloves of the deck crew who also use the handrails. It is akin to hair on the barbershop floor.

Item: Yesterday as we were eating breakfast, the ship slowed, then came to a stop. For three hours it floated dead in the water, drifting with the wind. No one seemed alarmed and as time passed we learned that it was simply a routine stop required to perform engine maintenance.

Item: If there is one fault, and we always must find at least one fault, it is lack of information. I realize that this ship exists to transport cargo, not passengers, but with minimal effort the passengers who are accepted could be kept abreast of basic activities on board.

Item: The crew, at all levels, are gentlemen. In passing, they greet you in some manner, a smile, a wave, or a "Morning," still, they are professionals and have a job to do which does not include entertaining or teaching passengers. That is not to say that they do not engage in conversation but it tends to be on their terms. All the officers speak English; the others communicate as best they can. At all levels, the native tongue is used when speaking to each other.

Item: Thus far, seasickness has not been an issue. The ship has a gentle roll which conveys the feelings of strength and progress.

Item: Since Savannah we have had no news from the outside world. I am sure a major world event would be relayed to the ship via radio or satellite but barring that, there is absolutely no news. Both Reg and I have found that our short wave radios receive mostly static or limited reception in a foreign tongue. Frankly, I prefer the solitude of the sea.

Wed, Jan 28   16° 32′ 49″S
575 Mi. / 7635 Total Miles   147° 39′ 06″W

Land Ho! Off the port bow!

Our eight-day Pacific crossing is behind us. Stepping out on deck at 0610, I sighted land for the first time in five-thousand miles–but it was not Tahiti. A trip to the bridge confirmed that this was but a small island heralding the French Polynesian Archipelago. It would be eleven hours before docking at Tahiti but already maps on the navigation desk had been changed to a larger scale and the Tahitian flag lay waiting to be unfurled as we entered "her" port.

Before moving on I feel an urge to pay tribute to those early mariners who sailed these seas. We had a sturdy vessel, a professional crew, a freezer of food, unlimited fresh water, adequate fuel, and the most modern navigational equipment available. Throughout the ages, explorers, adventurers, and fools have set off in a questionable craft, with only minimal provisions, and the stars. Most of them completed a journey similar to ours. I salute them all.

At 1500 Tahiti finally appeared, not the tropical Shangri-la pictured in guidebooks, but an island  shrouded in fog being drenched by the first significant rainfall of our trip. Within moments a pilot was on board guiding us into a small harbor within easy walking distance of town and within an hour, passport in hand, I was on my way.

My sister Jessica and I had visited Papeete in 1996 and not much has changed. I remembered it as a scruffy little town and was not disappointed. Downtown consists of four or five blocks spread along the harbor with a busy thoroughfare separating a small waterfront park from tourist shops, restaurants, and bars. Only a few blocks deep, the buildings quickly change from commercial to residential and begin to climb the steep volcanic slopes. Little cars, big trucks, and the ubiquitous moped clog the narrow streets crushing what charm Papeete may have once had.

The hour was late, most of the stores were closed, and I could not buy a phone card to call Marise, so I returned to the ship and for the first time watched it self-unload.

Thu, Jan 29   16° 32' 13"S
146 Mi. / 7781 Total Miles   149° 34' 29"W

Top priority for today was to call Marise. As I passed the small French Naval Station on my early walk into town I heard a rooster crowing. Yesterday's fog was gone but perpetual clouds hung over the mountain peaks behind Papeete. Our day was going to be hot. The post office air conditioning was welcome as I waited in the twenty-minute line to buy a phone card and stamps.

Card in hand, I headed for a phone only to be stymied by instructions in French. The French must love French; they allow nothing else. Off to the visitor center where a sweet young damsel finally got me through to the U.S., only to get our answering service. Call later.

The French Navy

Containers and Kayacks

I wandered over to the town market. Alongside the expected woven baskets and scarves was a tempting palette of fresh vegetables, fruit, fish, and flowers. A large tourist ship was in the harbor and many of its passengers were drifting through the aisles seeking that special memento that would memorialize their trip to Tahiti. Meanwhile, at the produce section local women were spending equal time looking for nutrients for their family that would disappear by nightfall.

Fashion   *Fruit*

My purchases included a pair of sandals, some AAA batteries, and a placemat. My one vice is collecting cheap placemats with gaudy pictures of our destinations, captured forever under a film of plastic. I have over one hundred of these tacky mementoes and have threatened Marise with the thought of plastering "my" room with them if we ever settle down. They are lightweight, easy to store, and cheap. That is until Tahiti. Never have I paid more than $3.00 but today I paid almost twice that. The picture of a beautiful maiden paddling her canoe into the golden-pacific sunset was so tasteless that I had to have it. Incidently, gasoline cost $2.10 per liter ($8.00 per gal.) and Carl paid $12.00 for a copy of *The Economist*.

Normally, while on shore leave I don't spend time eating, preferring to see the sights rather than sit in a restaurant. However, this morning I craved a cup of coffee and where better to get quick service then the Golden Arches. True to its reputation, everything was the same except the French menu, but everyone understands "coffee."

At 1100 I again called Marise and this time got through. After two weeks we quickly used up the twenty-minute phone card. We live a close life in our RV and I already miss those idle conversations. And she may be regretting her secret wish that I "shape up or ship out."

By this time Papeete was hot and humid. I briefly met Reg and Lynne and even they, who are staunch walkers, decided to enjoy the park for a while. Papeete's waterside park is its saving grace. An open plaza surrounded by large shade trees, it provides a cool retreat with a view of the harbor. Last night a small band was strumming out its lilting tropical rhythms as I passed through.

Deciding to have one more look around before returning to the *Manet*, I headed back across the main boulevard toward the quieter back streets. Before long I was attracted by the sound of another rhythm but unlike last night, this had a hard driving island beat to it. The sound emanated from the "Association Philanthropic Chinese," a large-open building of Chinese style. Gingerly I walked in and found two dozen women doing their morning exercise as a form of tropical line dancing. Not seemingly bothered by my presence, even occasionally smiling at me, I retreated from the heat to enjoy their beat for a few moments.

It was time to return to the *Manet* for a cold shower.

Noumea, New Caledonia, and Tahiti are the only two ports we will visit that do not have gantry cranes to transfer containers. Here we must use the ship's three cranes which can lift and lower just as quickly but don't have the ability to position containers like the land-based gantry cranes. Positioning here is an art form.

As each container is lifted suspended from the crane's single strand, it tends to slowly revolve. Arriving at its allotted space, it must be subdued, then pushed and prodded to an exact point so that when the crane operator sets it down, it will lock into the container below.

This positioning is done by men who perform a ballet as beautiful to watch as the Bolshoi. Situated seventy feet off the ground, these dancers coax, cajole, and coerce each giant box into its final resting place. Using hand signals to the operator, extreme agility, and brute force, they tame these thirty-ton boxes and lock them in their cage.

Occupational Safety and Health Administration (OSHA) would have an instant stroke if they saw these man-monkeys leap between containers, often at the edge of nowhere, and always without a hand rail. Like iron workers on a skyscraper, they do their job with a grace that makes it appear casual. It isn't.

By 1700 the pilot was on board and our tug was turning us about to head back out to the Pacific. Twenty miles west of Tahiti is the Island of Moorea. Turning to our new course, the *Manet* proceeded south toward New Zealand, passing Moorea at dusk.

Fri, Jan 30   20° 29' 35"S
398 Mi. / 8173 Total Miles   154° 42' 39'W

Because this is a freighter, there is no entertainment on board; no floor shows, no gambling, no night clubs. We must entertain ourselves. Pancha was in the middle of her seventh book when I interrupted them for this photo. Reg watched all three episodes of *The God Father*, Lynne loves to look at the stars, and Carl works wonders on his computer. I devote much of my time to writing this book, but having an hour to fill this afternoon, I decided that rather then putting a puzzle together, I would watch *The Battle Between Bow and Breaker.*

One of the joys of going to sea is "sea watching." Just as we like to "people watch," out here a favorite pastime for all of us is sea watching. This afternoon conditions were ideal. A stiff wind was whipping the ocean surface into five-foot waves creating occasional whitecaps as they crossed our path. The *Manet* was in fine shape as she plowed ahead under a brilliant sky, driven by her massive prop. Perfect conditions for an all-out, knock-down fight, and I had a ringside seat.

Just off the main deck, one hundred feet aft of the bow, the contestants were loosening up. In one corner we had the sea. Its trainer, the wind, had lashed him into top shape as he danced around the ring occasionally flashing a white scowl. He was full of energy, robust and eager to make his mark as he rolled forward into battle. Meanwhile, the *Manet* had its work cut out. She was the clear favorite, weighing in at a respectable thirty-thousand tons against a pitiful lightweight, but she was handicapped with her responsibility to reach port on time. Now she had to fight off this additional challenge.

A flying fish, acting as referee, sprinted between bow and breaker introducing the fighters. Bout time had arrived. The wind whistled and the battle began. Wearing vivid blue trunks, in came the hulking sea, a rolling, churning, powerhouse, smashing into *Manet's* bow with a crushing blow reverberating throughout the ship. Wave was intent on taking out his opponent with the first swing but clearly he had underestimated his rival. He staggered as bow, unfazed by the blow, hurled him back in a massive, curling, white crescendo of foam and fury. Stunned and splattered in every direction on a blue canvas, in infinite patterns and shapes, the white wave lay dazed, fighting to regain his composure. As the ship slid by in disdainful scorn the wave tried to recover, but this once proud, warrior was flattened. A boiling caldron of froth and foam was all that remained. Billions of gossamer bubbles, struggling to gain the surface scrambled to reform and re-attack but to no avail. The wave lay dying on the canvas. Too groggy to resist, he vanished forever in *Manet's* wake, the mop-up half of her one-two punch.

Manet proudly plunged on having won a decisive victory over the wave, now dissolved into oblivion. The battle is over—no contest the referee declares, and we prepare to leave our seats. But wait, out there, fifty yards off the port side, another scrappy wave is taking shape, flexing its muscles, gaining intensity, preparing for battle . . .

Sat, Jan 31   24° 53' 35"S
583 Mi. / 8756 Total Miles   162° 31' 11"W

Time Zones

The earliest timekeeper was a stick, stuck in the sand somewhere in the mist of history. As the stick's shadow passed a certain point on the ground, it became a clock. Let's jump ahead a few thousand years. Now we have ornate clocks that keep reasonable time, but they are much too expensive for the average person and who needs a clock anyway? You get up with the chickens and go to bed when the chores are done.

Now let's jump again, this time to the 1830's. The telegraph has been invented, railroads are being built, and most people have a mass-produced watch which is both cheap and fairly accurate. Now John in New York can telegraph Mary in San Francisco telling her that he will arrive on the six o'clock train and they will go out to dinner. Mary gets dressed for dinner, goes to pick John up at the train station and gets mad when she looks at her watch at seven, and still no John. Finally John arrives and they have a big fight when he says that by his watch, which he set in New York, it is six o'clock, he is right on time.

In steps our hero Cleveland Abbe, a meteorologist who developed a time zone system with the earth's 360 degrees divided into twenty-four zones, one for each hour of the day. Divide 360 by 24 and you get 15, the degrees of longitude in each time zone.

However, time zones are of no value unless we know where the boundaries are. In the 1830's the British Empire ruled the world so they said, "We will run the first boundary from the north pole to the south pole. That line will pass right through our Royal Greenwich Observatory, and we will call it the Prime Meridian."

If you travel east from the prime meridian, you set your clock ahead one hour each time you cross a time zone line. If you travel west from the prime meridian, you set your clock back one hour each time you cross a time zone line. After going through twelve time zones in either direction you get to the International Date Line (IDL) where you jump over a day in the westerly direction or repeat a day in the easterly direction.

Let's illustrate with this trip. We left New York which is at Greenwich Mean Time (GMT)–5 hrs. Since then we have traveled through seven time zones and set our clock back seven times adding seven hours to our life. Now we are at GMT–12 hrs.

Today is Saturday, January 31. The moment we cross the IDL it will be Monday, February 2; we will actually jump over Sunday and loose twenty-four hours from our life. But as we continue our journey we will pass through seventeen more time zones, setting our clock back one hour each time, gaining one hour back in our life each time. This means that when we reach New York we will have gained the day back that we lost at the IDL(17+7=24 hrs.). We lost one day all at once when we crossed the IDL but we gained twenty-four hours one zone at a time as we traveled around the globe.

Advance one day

Retard one hour

To complicate matters slightly, time zone lines are not straight. Each country has the right to set them as they please and most countries bend them around geographical and political areas so that a city won't be cut in half by a time zone line. China, which covers five time zones, chooses to have all its people adhere to Beijing time. The United States covers eight time zones. Atlantic, Eastern, Central, Mountain, Pacific, Alaska, Hawaii, and Samoa. In which one do you live?

So now when John calls Mary, he says " I will be in on the six o'clock train, pacific time." They meet, have dinner, and you can finish the story.

While you are thinking of a diabolical ending, I am going to wrap up this chapter and put it to bed on the CD. Cheerio! Enjoy your Sunday, I'll see you on Monday on the Tasman Sea.

CHAPTER FOUR

Tasman Sea
⇒ Auckland ⇒ Noumea ⇒ Sydney ⇒

Mon, Feb 2   24° 53′ 33″S
613 Mi. / 9369 Total Miles   171° 02′ 23″W

Good Morning. Did you have a pleasant Sunday? We have a new day, new month, new chapter, and a new sea. Tasman Sea lies between New Zealand and Australia and is named for the Dutch explorer, Able Tasman. We will be floating around Mr. Tasman's sea for twelve days and visiting three ports, two of which I have been to, Auckland and Sydney. I know you will enjoy them.

Before getting started, there is one bit of leftover business. On January 30th, we crossed the Tropic of Capricorn. It was not a big deal, but I wrote a piece about it which I hate to waste. Let me slip it in here, then I promise, no more parallels of latitude.

With little fanfare, we crossed the Tropic of Capricorn yesterday. Not as significant as the equator, it is a parallel of latitude which encircles the earth at 23° 27′ south of the equator and represents the southernmost point where the sun appears directly overhead at least one day a year. This occurs at noon on December 22 each year and it is called the "summer solstice." It marks the beginning of summer in the southern hemisphere. Today is January 31, the temperature is 84° and we are experiencing the hottest part of summer.

The exact opposite occurs in the northern hemisphere. There, the line is called the Tropic of Cancer, and at 23° 27′N, it runs through Mexico and between Florida and Cuba. It marks the northernmost point where the sun appears overhead at noon on June 22 each year. This means that in the United States, the sun is never directly overhead because we are north of the Tropic of Cancer.

Our seasons are the result of the earth's axis being tilted at, you guessed it, 23° 27″. If the earth's axis were vertical in relation to the sun there would be no summer or winter, which means no summer vacations. Three cheers for tilt!

Two other parallels of latitude that we should mention, even though we will not cross them, are the Arctic and Antarctic Circles. They mark the furthest point from the poles in the Northern and

Southern hemispheres where, for at least one day each year, the sun does not appear above the horizon.

Because my computer skills are limited, I cannot round or tilt my earth, so please, use your imagination. Thanks, Bob.

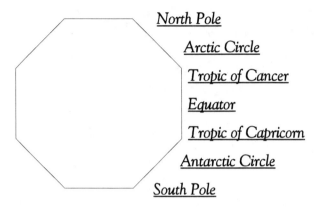

North Pole

Arctic Circle

Tropic of Cancer

Equator

Tropic of Capricorn

Antarctic Circle

South Pole

Tue, Feb 3   33° 28′ 14″S
522 Mi. / 9891 Total Miles   178° 36′ 26″W

Which shirt should I put on this morning? There are days when that is my most difficult decision. I have now been at sea long enough to have developed a daily routine. Let's walk through it.

Time varies because we keep setting the clock back, but before dawn I slip on a pair of shorts, go out on deck, and check the sunrise prospects. I keep hoping for one of those fabled south pacific sunrises where a huge tawny sun breaks through a horizon of puffy white clouds, turning the world to gold. It has yet to happen. Sometimes, if the wind is right, I savor the aroma of fresh bread baking in the galley.

Back in the cabin an hour is spent doing the morning chores. Performing pushups on a rolling ship can be an interesting experience. Breakfast is at seven and I try to arrive early for a brief chat with Criss and Danny, our Filipino cook. This morning he was proud of his pork rinds that had been fried for some future dish. Not my idea of breakfast food. My normal fare is juice, cereal, yogurt, a piece of fresh bread, and tea. Available for the more hardy are eggs, bacon, toast, and occasionally pancakes. A tray of fresh fruit is always nearby.

Around 0815 I move up to the bridge to check our location on the always present charts. The officers stand watch as follows:

1st Mate 0400 to 0800 and 1600 to 2000
2nd Mate 0800 to 1200 and 2000 to 2400
3rd Mate 1200 to 1600 and 2400 to 0400

At 0815, the second mate, a Filipino, is always cordial but not very talkative so I usually return in the afternoon when the first mate (chief officer), a Croatian, is on duty.

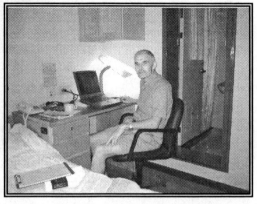

By 0830 I am at my desk working on this book. The writing is fairly easy; it's the picture adaptation and computer technology that is time consuming. On more then one occasion Carl has rescued me from a computer crash and I am grateful. Criss comes in at 0900 to give the room a quick clean. This morning he told me about the prior occupant of this cabin, a gentleman of my age who had lost his wife. Just before 1000 I take the daily latitude and longitude readings. At home I never have coffee after breakfast, but here, on this ship, I am like one of Pavlov's dogs; I can't wait for ten o'clock coffee and three small butter cookies. Sometimes with ease, sometimes with anguish, the morning speeds by as I print these precious words to paper.

Noontime finds the five of us gathered around the dining table sharing tidbits of news about the ship or solving the world's problems. We tend to agree but do not shy from disagreement. As usual, political topics seem to agitate. Lynne and Reg have their problems with Tony Blair. Pancha and Carl tend to support George Bush and I strongly support their right to be wrong.

After lunch I always don my hard hat and visit the bow. The bow is my chapel and I will tell you more as time permits. After an hour of sea watching I return to the cabin for more writing or housekeeping chores. I am a Klutz at washing clothes, writing postcards, things that Marise does so well. Between 1600 and 1700 I am at the gym rowing or bicycling away the calories put on at lunch. Then a shower, and before dinner, another trip to the bridge.

The chief officer is a thirty-six-year-old who is the most approachable of all the officers. He has a wealth of knowledge about the ship and future ports. When he starts promoting Croatia, watch out, he is very partisan. An avid photographer, he uses a camera similar to mine. Yesterday I gave him some photos of the *Manet* taken at Tahiti.

At 1800 we sit down to another delicious dinner and hour of chit chat. Then it's out on deck for a check of the weather and more sea watching. When the spirit moves, I retire to my cabin for more writing. This book takes up much of my time. There are nights when I get up at 0300 and work for a few hours.

Other then at mealtimes, we passengers do not mingle much. Reg and Lynne can always be found lounging in the sun with a book, or simply wave watching. They often go to the gym for a game of ping pong and I occasionally see Reg watching a late-night movie in the lounge. Carl and Pancha read a lot. When they leave at Auckland, they will double the ship's library with their books left behind. They also play a lot of Scrabble and use my dictionary to settle occasional controversies.

With minimal outside influence, a daily routine becomes inevitable. Woe be to the passenger who depends on others to fill their time. He will jump ship after the second day out.

PS: The map shows that tonight could be the night we fall off the edge of the earth.   Sleep tight!

Wed, Feb 4   36° 50' 40"S
440 Mi. / 10331 Total Miles   174° 47' 02"E

It has been a long day with highs and lows, but before we ride the roller coaster, look at today's heading. We passed the ten-thousand-mile mark, and our longitude reading has changed from West to East. Now it will slowly decrease as we continue westward.

Auckland, New Zealand–with tongue-in-cheek, Reg and Lynne, our English friends, said they were disappointed because it was so much like their home. Auckland is a charming city, cosmopolitan, and just the right size.

I first saw the reflection of its lights on the clouds at 0300, when we were far out at sea. I was up and down three times during the night to watch the city take shape, as we drew closer. By the time the first line was secured to a bollard at 0600, the clouds had turned to a light, but steady rain.

This was the day that Carl and Pancha were leaving our small group, so our last breakfast was rather mushy. I gave them an autographed copy of my first book, a small token for all the help and encouragement they gave me toward this work. We shall miss them.

By 0930, having gotten wet walking the mile into town, I had exchanged some dollars and bought an umbrella. At the visitor center I obtained a map of the town and purchased a phone card. This time the directions were in English and there was no problem getting through to Marise. She seems to be having a ball. Her childhood friend, Louise, is visiting the RV for two weeks, and when I called, they were both enjoying a visit with Jessica and Jim in Deland, Florida.

So here I am, abandoned by Carl and Pancha, all but forgotten by those at home, and soaking wet. Poor me, dejected and down in the dumps. What to do?

Obvious—you soar to the top of the tallest tower in the southern hemisphere and have a cup of coffee.

Sky Tower is over one thousand feet high and pierces the sky like a needle sprouting out of Auckland's center. On a clear day you can see fifty miles, east to the Pacific and west to the Tasman. But this was not a clear day, so after warming up and drying out I walked around the observation platform. At several points there are glass panels embedded in parts of the floor. I had to summon all my courage to walk across, viewing the city's streets far below.

There are two other interesting activities associated with Sky Tower; both require more bravery and a fatter wallet than I have. You can "Sky Jump" from the tower attached to one of its cables, but don't ask me how they slow you down at the bottom, or you can do the "Vertigo Climb." Escorted and harnessed, you climb inside the topmost needle and then exit to a small crow's nest. Hang on tight! Revived and refreshed, I descended to the streets of Auckland.

Sophisticated and stylish would be appropriate adjectives to describe Auckland. Even on a rainy day, dark business suits and dresses are common on Queen Street, and being the height of the tourist season, backpackers and other travelers crowded the small downtown. After a month of ship cuisine, I had a Mac attack, then wandered down to the harbor.

In the 1995 America's Cup Race, *Black Magic* from New Zealand defeated the *Stars & Stripes* crew on *Young America* to become the first yacht from this country to win the trophy. As you can imagine, black is a popular T shirt color.

By 1600 it was time to head home to the *Manet*. Finally the sun was beginning to poke through and I reached for my sunglasses. That's funny, I thought I brought them—they must be back on my desk. Not so. The roller coaster hit bottom. Somewhere, back there in Auckland, lay my prescription sunglasses, probably pulled out of my shirt pocket when I reached for something else.

Roller coasters always end at the bottom.

Thu, Feb 5	32° 37′ 36″S
310 Mi. / 10641 Total Miles	172° 53′ 08″E

Yesterday on the streets of Auckland we saw skin of every shade. Sixty-two percent of European decent, fourteen percent Pacific Island, thirteen percent Asian, and eleven percent Maori; it is a microcosm of our world.

We, the People

The preamble to the constitution of the United States begins: We, the People of the United States . . . Let me temporarily change those first words to We, the People of the World. Let's take a look at all of us, from every continent, country, and corner of the earth.

The World Almanac places the world population in year 2000 at 6,080,000,000 and we are distributed around the globe as follows:

WORLD POPULATION

Asia	3,688,000,000
Africa	805,000,000
Europe	729,000,000
North America	481,000,000
South America	347,000,000

Oceania (South Pacific) 31,000,000
Antarctica, which accounts for nearly ten percent of the earth's land surface has no permanent population.

We live in 181 sovereign countries, the most populated being.
MOST POPULATED COUNTRIES
China 1,273,000,000
India 1,030,000,000
United States 278,000,000
Indonesia 229,000,000
Brazil 175,000,000
Vatican City has the world's smallest population with fewer than 1,000 citizens and also the smallest size, 110 acres.

We speak in more than 200 tongues which are localized by thousands of dialects.
MOST COMMON LANGUAGES
Mandarin (China) 885,000,000
English 450,000,000
Hindi (India) 367,000,000
Spanish 352,000,000
Russian 294,000,000
Arabic 202,000,000

Unfortunately, one half the world's population cannot read or write. The top 20% of us receive 75% of the world's annual wages while the bottom 20% receive 2%.

We follow countless religious faiths, but more than one fifth of the world's people remain nonbelievers.
MAJOR RELIGIONS
Christian 1,999,000,000
Muslim 1,188,000,000
Hindu 811,000,000
Chinese folk religions 384,000,000
Buddhist 360,000,000
Jewish 14,000,000

After looking at all these figures you might think that We, the People are a very diverse group. However, if we view humanity through a different lens, there is only one attribute that makes us dissimilar. Fifty-one percent of us are females and forty-nine percent of us are males.

Fri, Feb 6   32° 37' 36"S
546 Mi. / 11187 Total Miles   168° 20' 01"E

Weather has changed our routine for today. We have left the low pressure area that gave us rain in Auckland and we are now in a high pressure zone with clear skies and strong winds. When I tried to go to the bow this afternoon, one of the deckhands shooed me off, saying it was too dangerous. Instead, let's stay indoors and take a tour of the superstructure, circled below.

Take all the containers and the three cranes off the ship, and the only thing you will see above deck is the superstructure. It is where the crew eats, sleeps, and for the most part, controls the ship.

When you walk up the gangplank, you enter the ship on the cargo deck, which we will cover on a later day. Above the cargo deck there are seven decks including the Bridge. Starting at Deck A at the bottom, up to Deck F which is topped by the Bridge. Each deck is similar in design and construction but as you will see, each has a separate function.

On this ship each member of the crew has a private room and bath. Criss is responsible for cleaning the rooms on Deck E and F, but all other crew members clean their own rooms. Each level has a floor plan with room assignment by title or usage and the lower the title, the lower the room.

A Deck: Refrigerator chambers, Provision stores, Stewards stores, Air conditioning machinery room, Dirty Linen, Ship's office and Deck workshop.

B Deck: Officer's smoking room, Officer's mess, Officer's pantry, Galley, Crew's mess, and Crew's recreation room.

C Deck: Able Seaman quarters A – J, Crew's laundry, and Drying room.

D Deck: 3rd Officer, Boatswain, Officer's spare, Asst. Engineer, Cook, Asst. Electrical, 4th Engineer, 3rd Engineer, Officer's spare, Officer's laundry, and Drying room.

E Deck: Chief Officer, Officer's spare, Conference room, Owner's cabin, 2nd Engineer, and Supercargo.

F Deck: Master's day room and bedroom, Administrative office, Pilot, and Chief Engineer's day room and bedroom.

Bridge: Control room

There is a small elevator but the passengers seldom use it. A typical day requires a passenger to travel from his cabin on E to B Deck three times for meals, E to the Cargo Deck, and E to the Bridge at least once. Most passengers would consider that a bare minimum.

Sat, Feb 7   22° 15' 51"S
271 Mi. / 11458 Total Miles   166° 25' 50"E

Noumea, New Caledonia is going to be a tough town to write about. It has few endearing attributes. The central park is nice, the flora is spectacular, but don't travel eleven thousand miles just to visit Noumea.

If these pictures were in color, you would see the brilliant orange of the flower, or the jade green of this enormous tree. Anywhere else, this beauty would be a prime specimen; here it simply shades a parking lot.

Our approach to Noumea was similar to that of Auckland. The *Manet* tied up in the rain at about 0600, just as we had three days ago in New Zealand. This time I delayed my walk into town until the rain stopped. I still got wet. In Auckland I got wet with rain; in Noumea I got wet with sweat. Around 1000, the sun broke through the clouds creating a sauna and sending me back to the ship for short pants and a hat.

Our ship was docked just a few blocks from the town center so I decided to stay on board for lunch. The captain and I were the only ones eating, everyone else apparently occupied, or in town. He said that he had some French francs left over from Tahiti which he wanted to spend before leaving.

When I returned in the afternoon, I had no francs and didn't care to pay the steep conversion fee for changing money, so I just drifted. Other than the park, Noumea has little to offer. It is the kind of town where all the postcards are aerial shots so you don't see details. Being the center of government and commerce for New Caledonia, it is a working town, and since this was Saturday afternoon, no one was working. The only activity of interest was a chess match in the park.

At one shop I tried to buy a placemat but surprisingly, they would not accept U.S. dollars. As I walked back to the ship, I speculated that without a placemat for my "wall of travel," Noumea would quickly be forgotten.

Sun, Feb 8   23° 59' 55"S
183 Mi. / 11641 Total Miles   164° 14' 35"E

The fact that we are not on a cruise ship was made crystal clear this morning. As 1000 approached I was looking forward to a cup of coffee and the usual three butter cookies. When I met Lynne in the lounge, she was not smiling, rare for her. Criss had told her that we had run out of butter cookies, and the substitute would be saltine crackers. We couldn't help but laugh, wondering what would happen if that occurred on the Queen Mary 2. The steward would be thrown overboard.

This being a quiet Sunday after our exciting day in Noumea, it might be a good time to cover some more minor topics.

Item : Other than the butter cookie bust, the food has been good. Not gourmet, but substantial and good, suitable for a crew of men at any work station. As noted earlier, we eat in the officer's mess with the only difference being a carafe of wine on the passenger's table. The remainder of the crew eat in a separate dining room from a different menu, which I believe is slanted toward their Filipino tastes.

Food stores are replenished at Savannah, Auckland, Singapore, and Rotterdam. And I'm sure that fresh produce, and hopefully butter cookies are brought on board at other ports.

Item: For other "necessities," there is always the Slop Chest. To purchase from the Slop Chest, you fill out a form and Danny will deliver the item to your room. You are billed monthly or when leaving the ship, and pay with U.S. dollars. Here are some representative prices of the forty-three items presently stocked.

Marlboro Red/ Lights	$12.69/ ctn
Coca-cola	9.33 / cs
Mineral water	4.74 / cs
Crown Reserve	7.34 / btl
Table wine Spanish 1ltr	0.81 / cask
Old Spice Deodorant stick 75ml	5.22 /st
Toothbrush Jordan	0.97 / pc
Colgate toothpaste	1.53 / tube
Letter envelopes, 10in.	0.70 / pkt
Writing pad	1.44 / pad
Pringles potato chips	2.17 / tube
Mixed nuts 150gr	2.24 / tin
Vodka .75ltr	7.35 / btl
Jack Daniel's 75cl	16.80 /btl
Beck's beer in bottles	15.39 / cs
Cadbury Chocolate 250gms	3.12 /bar

Item: Today being Sunday we will probably be offered pancakes at breakfast, steak at the noon meal, and ice cream for desert.

Item: Just in case you are deeply involved in some difficult task, or sleeping, the ship blows its horn every day exactly at noon so you won't miss all this good food.

Mon, Feb 9   29° 37' 36"S
586 Mi. / 12227 Total Miles   157° 08' 05"E

Monday morning, the beginning of our fifth week at sea, time to take stock. After leaving New York, we traveled down the east coast, through the Carribean Sea and Panama Canal. Then eight days across the Pacific to Tahiti, southwest to New Zealand followed by a little detour north to Noumea. Incidently, we probably would not have gone out of our way except that Noumea is a territory of France and this is The French Line. Now we are headed southwest again.

For the next ten days we will be sailing in Australian waters and visiting four Australian cities. Let's take a brief look at Australia, the Country. The correct title is the Commonwealth of Australia. Prior to 1931, like many other countries, it was part of the British Empire. In that year, the British Parliament proclaimed

the Commonwealth a free association of self-governing nations, united by a common allegiance to the Crown.

Strange as it seems, Australia was settled partly because of the American Revolution. Before the Revolution, Britain had exiled its criminals and other undesirables to the Colonies. With America no longer available, Britain looked to the Pacific for a penal colony in the "remote and unattractive" land of Australia. In 1786, seven hundred convicts were expelled to Port Jackson, today known as Sydney, one of the most beautiful harbors in the world. Reg says that now it is considered a badge of honor to be a direct descendant of one of those early criminals.

Australia is the smallest continent and the sixth largest country. It is four-fifths the size of the U.S., and divided into six states. It is one of the world's flattest land masses, averaging one thousand feet above sea level. Most of the interior, known as the outback, is sparsely populated.

At the center of Australia there is a strange geological formation called Ayers Rock. It is the largest monolith in the world, with a base circumference of six miles, and rising 1143 feet out of the flat desert floor. Jessica and I had the good fortune, along with hundreds of other tourists, to climb Ayers Rock in 1996.

Today, Ayers Rock is known as Uluru because of its importance to the Aborigines. Long before the convicts, possibly fifty thousand years ago, Aboriginal people migrated to Australia from southeast Asia. Primarily nomadic, they lived off the land for centuries increasing to a population of three-hundred thousand by the time of the first white settlers. As with the American Indians, those numbers dramatically fell to sixty thousand by 1920 due to disease, social disruption, and brutal mistreatment. As late as the 1971 census, they were not even counted. Since then their lot has improved somewhat. Aboriginal culture is now expressed in art, music, and sport.

Today Australia has a population of twenty million, less then ten percent of the U.S.. Eighty percent of its citizens are concentrated on just three percent of its land, mostly along the southeast coast. Ninety percent are of European descent and English is the official language. Australia is self-sufficient in food, and exports large quantities of wheat, meat, dairy products, and wool. The country is also rich in minerals, exporting iron ore and gold. To sweeten the pot, they are also the world's largest producers of diamonds, producing two-fifths of the global total. Tourism has become a major business, and we will contribute our share of the five billion dollars earned each year.

That is just a brief outline of the country we will visit next week. See you there for a detailed walkabout.

Tue, Feb 10   33° 58' 17"S
458 Mi. / 12685 Total Miles   151° 12' 47"E

Now that's more like it. Sydney has more to see than we could dream of covering in one day, but we hit the highlights, leaving the details for when you come back on your own someday.

Our day began at 0300 when on a whim, I took a look outside. Ten miles off our starboard side I caught the first glimpse of light from the Continent of Australia, probably a light house. Three hours later we were tied up, not in Sydney Harbor as we had hoped, but in Botany Bay where all the container ships now go. This turned out to be a blessing in disguise.

There is a standard ritual when the *Manet* enters a new port. Before anything else happens, there is a meeting in the conference room attended by the master, customs agents, and the port agent who represents CMA CGM, the shipping company. During that meeting Customs reviews the paperwork for freight, and passports for passengers and crew, and they all have coffee. Only after everything is in order are the passengers given their passports and allowed to leave.

Botany Bay is about ten miles from downtown Sydney and this morning, after the meeting, the port agent volunteered to give Reg, Lynne, and me a ride into town saving us taxi fare. Our ride into town turned out to be a fully narrated, personal tour of suburban Sydney, including a stop at Bondi Beach, Australia's famous surf beach, where we all had a second cup of coffee. At 1000 Rob dropped three grateful passengers off in downtown Sydney and we got our first look at a sight definitely worth traveling twelve thousand miles for.

The Sydney Opera House and Sydney Harbor Bridge are recognized throughout the travel world as destinations not to be missed. Completed in 1973 after the resignation of its original architect, the opera complex includes the opera and ballet theater, a concert hall, a theater for small plays, and a cinema. Every New Year's Eve you see the Sydney Harbor Bridge, better known as the Coat Hanger, draped with a waterfall of fireworks that seems to fall forever. Both are Kodak Moments.

These two landmarks are located on either side of the Circular Quay, a hub for tourists and Sydney's transportation. From here, ferries fan out to a dozen harbor ports, and buses circulate to every local neighborhood. On this day, it is the perfect spot for lunch and people watching. Chained to the ships schedule, I dallied as long as I dared but then it was time to take care of personal business.

First order of business was to call Marise which required the purchase of a local phone card. That was no problem but once again I was unable to get through, so left a message telling her that all was well. Then it was off to replace the sunglasses that disappeared in Auckland. I was directed to a store with an in-house lab but it was too late in the day for same-day pickup so I bought a pair of generic glasses.

If I had known then what I know now, I could have gotten prescription glasses. When I returned to the ship this evening, I learned that due to loading problems, shore leave had been extended to 1400, Wednesday. C'est la vie. That's life.

Wed, Feb 11   Same
Same   Same

When we left off yesterday, we were attending to personal business, namely shopping and a haircut. I was running out of paper for the printer; no problem, just go to Office Depot and buy a ream, right? Not here. It is easy to find a stationary store but not so easy to find the right size paper. In Australia the common size is A4 (8.3" x 11.7"). The store manager finally found some 8.5" x 11" but it cost eleven dollars, more then twice what we would pay at home. Yet then again, maybe it was the store?

QVB stands for Queen Victoria Building. It is wonderfully described as " . . . an experience of grand proportions where history, culture, and shopping converge under a majestic dome." This ain't no Wal-Mart. Five levels of glitter and glitz right in the heart of Sydney. It is the only shopping center I know of that offers guided tours.

For fifty years Marise has cut my hair but with her being half a world away, I had to revert to Sasha. Talented and talkative, she restored my natural beauty but I dare not tell Marise the price she got.

With business out of the way it was time to see the sights of Sydney, and there is no better spot for that than the Coat Hanger. The day had grown warm but I walked across the bridge, slowly soaking in the sights. From that vantage point you can see the harbor, the opera house, Sydney Tower, The Rocks–Sydney's birthplace, Darling Harbor, the Royal Botanic Gardens, and Sydney itself.

Finally it was time to head home and for the first time I made use of the Flying Angels, formally known as the Mission of Seafarers. "The Mission of Seafarers is a world mission agency of the Anglican Church which cares for the practical and spiritual needs of seafarers of all nationalities and faiths." All too often it is thought of as simply a seaman's shuttle service between port and town, but it also provides inexpensive rest and relaxation for seamen in a strange port far from home. Most ports have a local branch and it was there that I went to get a ride back to Botany Bay.

Back on board, I was greeted with two pleasant surprises. The first was the delay of the ship, and while an extra day may be pleasant for me, each day costs CMA CGM eighty thousand dollars, so I am sure the master held a different view. My second pleasure was meeting our new passenger, Lia. A woman in her fifties of Dutch nationality, she is experienced in freighter travel to the extent of bringing her own folding bicycle for travel in ports. Prior to boarding the *Manet*, she traveled on its sister ships, the CMA CGM *Matisse* and *La Tour*. She is going to Malta and we will get to know her better as the trip progresses.

And the trip is progressing. As I write this, the departure time has been set back six more hours to 2000. But at some point we will slip our lines and proceed at half speed through Botany Bay. Beyond that, freed from delay and restriction, the first mate will call for full sea speed as he retires the Tasman Sea chart for the Southern Ocean.

CHAPTER FIVE

Southern Ocean

⇒ Melbourne ⇒ Adelaide ⇒ Perth ⇒

Thu, Feb 12   36° 06′ 23″S
151 Mi. / 12836 Total Miles   150° 39′ 26″E

One month ago we entered a new world. Today we are almost halfway around it. At 0300 the last container was put in place and within minutes we were on our way, twenty-one hours behind schedule. The *Manet* is now headed almost due south within sight of Australia's east coast. Sometime later today we will change to a westerly heading, beginning our week-long passage south of Australia.

Did you notice that in this first paragraph I spoke of time and direction knowing that all my readers would understand? This world would be a better place if I could do the same with length, volume, and weight.

Weights and Measures

As we move farther from the U.S. and experience new cultures, two thoughts come to mind. What a wonderful country we live in, and what a dumb system of weights and measures we use. The whole world uses the metric system, yet we still cling to the antiquated foot, pound, and gallon. Properly defined, a foot is part of the anatomy, a pound is a place for stray dogs, and only heaven knows the origin of a gallon, but it equals 1/63 of a hogshead. Now that makes a lot of sense.

The U.S. has taken steps to convert to the metric system, with limited success. We run the hundred-meter dash and we drink our soda from liter bottles, so why can't we go all the way and measure our highways in kilometers.

In 1975 President Ford signed the Metric Conversion Act which would have, if carried out, simplified weights and measures, part of the basic fabric of life. Yet thirty years later we continue to resist. Science, medicine, the military, and even some sports, have adopted metric, so why can't the average Joe switch, or at least have his child learn metric in grade school.

Why is metric so much better than our old English system? Let's compare:

U.S.	Metric
	Length
12 inches = 1 foot	10 millimeters = 1 centimeter
3 feet = 1 yard	100 centimeters = 1 meter
5280 feet = 1 mile	1000 meters = 1 kilometer
	Volume
8 ounces = 1 cup	10 milliliters = 1 centiliter
4 cups = 1 quart	10 centiliters = 1 deciliters
4 quarts = 1 gallon	10 deciliters = 1 liter
	Weight
16 ounces = 1 pound	1000 grams = 1 kilogram
2000 pounds = 1 ton	1000 kilograms = 1 ton

It is obvious, metric is easier. All one has to do is learn meter, liter, gram, and a few prefixes. Like the dollar system we already use, the metric system is based on multiples of ten. On the other hand, the present U.S. system is based on arbitrary numbers and units which have no rhyme or reason.

When we use the term ounce, are we talking about 8 ounces of water or 16 ounces of spaghetti? Water is a volume, spaghetti is a weight, but we use the same term of measurement. Conversely, a gallon and a bushel are both measurements of volume but we use different terms.

Adoption of the metric system in the U.S. is inevitable. Just try to work on your car without a set of metric wrenches. The longer we resist, the more we lose out to worldwide competition. Ask any businessman who wants to sell his product overseas. He knows that:

0.6 miles = 1 kilometer
1.057 quarts = 1 liter
2.2 pounds = 1 kilogram

PS: Because this book was written for today's American audience, I have used the current U.S. system of Weights and Measures. In the second addition I would relish revising it to metric.

Fri, Feb 13   37° 48' 46"S
338 Mi. / 13174 Total Miles   144° 54' 42"E

Melancholy, that's how I felt most of the day, and as I mull over events, there are reasons for my mood. Weather was the first culprit. It dawned gray and chilly, forcing me to don long pants and a sweatshirt for the first time in weeks. The port agent was the second culprit. He sped right by as the four of us waited at the terminal gate for a ride into Melbourne. Unlike the gentlemen at Sydney, this fellow forced us to take a cab and later, at the dinner table, I was rightfully admonished for tipping the surly cab driver. Not a good start.

Usually I have a good sense of direction, but on this morning, even though I had been there before, I was disorientated in downtown Melbourne. Possibly because the sun, my compass, was not shining, or possibly because so much had changed. Even these three statues were of little help.

Lacking direction and purpose, I got a map at the visitor center and walked to the Queen Victoria Market, Melbourne's oldest and largest. But with nothing to purchase, I found little of interest among the one-thousand vendor stalls, and soon left.

One of the delights of Melbourne is the free City Circle Tram. Beginning with a horse drawn carriage in 1884, the city has provided continuous service covering most of the downtown area, and it was here that I finally got my bearings. After circling half the city I decided to hop off and go for a walk in Fitzroy Gardens at the east end of town. Here, among other attractions, you will find Cooks Cottage, the 1755 family home of Captain James Cook, a gift from England to the City of Melbourne. One unexpected monument which did nothing to brighten my mood was a memorial to John F. Kennedy.

It was time to call Marise, and I caught up with her as she and Louise were driving back to the RV from dinner with Iris, her sister, and Bert. The initial excitement of this trip has passed and I momentarily catch myself wishing to be back with Marise at gatherings like this.

One of the memories from my previous visit to Melbourne was the Shrine of Remembrance, and in my melancholy mood this seemed an appropriate place to visit next. The Shrine was originally built to honor those who died in the 1917 First World War, "the war to end all wars." That was not to be. In World War II one out of seven Australians actively served, and 27,073 were killed in action. An additional Cenotaph was dedicated by Her Majesty, Queen Elizabeth II on February 28, 1954, almost fifty years ago to the day. Unfortunately governments still war and commoners still die. Now the Shrine memorializes Australia's dead from all conflicts.

Centerpiece of the Sanctuary is a marble stone set below floor level where "no hands may touch it and where visitors must bow their heads to read the inscription." Each year on the eleventh day of the eleventh month, a sunray passes across the face of this stone and exactly at the eleventh hour it illuminates the word *LOVE*. I felt privileged to participate in the daily re-enactment of that annual event.

A second attraction of the Shrine of Remembrance is its location. Set on a high point of land and facing directly down Swanson Street, the main street of Melbourne, from its balcony there are spectacular views of the city. However, here again I was disappointed. First with the construction. In many directions, new buildings were blocking the skyline. I know that tax collectors see these boxes as streams of new revenue. I saw them as sacrilegious.

Second, and a more aggressive affront to the Shrine, is the new visitor center. Like a scar left by a wayward bomb, it neither matches nor complements the Shrine's architecture. If needed for security, secure it underground with a roof of grass. Even the guard with whom I spoke was apologetic for it.

Speaking of apologies, if I have depressed you with my blue day in Melbourne, I apologize. As I left the Shrine to return downtown, the haze and my spirits lifted. At 1700 we met back at the Seaman's Mission where they were kind enough to return us to the *Manet*.

Sat, Feb 14   38° 51′ 59″S
127 Mi. / 13301 Total Miles   142° 59′ 10″E

This morning we departed at 0330 leaving a fine city behind, despite my brooding of yesterday. At 0600 I was surprised to see the pilot still on board but the need for his experience soon became apparent. The west opening to Melbourne's harbor is a relatively narrow channel that creates a fast current during tide changes. This morning it was a new experience to see the powerful *Manet* struggle against what the first mate told me later was a seven-knot current.

This was a day of change. Having completed his current contract, Danny, the Radio Operator and passenger's liaison, left the ship last night. He is being replaced by Alfredo, and I was amused by my introduction. Danny presented me by my departure and destination cities, Mr. New York – New York.

The captain has been in full uniform all day anticipating his departure tomorrow at Adelaide. We wish him well. You will meet your new master as soon as I do.

There was a third change which will not become apparent until you check tomorrow's latitude. At some point during the day we reached our most southerly latitude and tomorrow the numbers will start going down as we slowly return north to zero at the equator. The reversal probably accrued as we passed between Australia and Tasmania, but unlike at the equator, no one was watching the GPS readout. We have traveled almost as far south of the equator as New York is north of the equator, not even halfway to the south pole.

Incidently, in the northern hemisphere, halfway to the north pole there lies a little town called Dexter, Maine. Marise was born there and when we were courting we would stop in at the *Forty-fifth Parallel Diner*. Now we have a cemetery plot in Dexter so our head stone will be at exactly latitude 45°N. How's that for planning?

Our day ended with one final change. Throughout this trip as we headed southwest, the sun, which sets in the west, would set off our starboard bow. Now we are headed in a northwest direction. Relative to the ship, where did the sun set this evening?

Sun, Feb 15   34° 46′ 11″S
376 Mi. / 13677 Total Miles   138° 29′ 20″E

I'm sorry folks. There is a limit to the sacrifices I will make for you. As we have moved around the world, I have researched cities, walked streets, and paid with time and coin in order to show you the highlights of each port, but today you ask too much.

Today, in order to show you the sights, I was forced to suffer the indignity of riding in a baby's car seat, and then plodding the streets of Adelaide on the hottest day in seventy years. Have mercy.

The car seat ride came about when the port agent offered us a lift to the train station. Actually I am proud to say that at my age, my hips still fit into a baby seat, allowing us all to squeeze into the car.

As you can see by the agent's paper, heat was today's topic. To convert 44.3 degrees Celsius to Fahrenheit, you multiply by 9/5, then add 32. On my calculator that equals 111.7 degrees on February 15th! And probably in Dexter, Maine which is a similar distance from the north pole as we are from the south pole, it was near 0 degrees. Why? All because of tilt. Remember the earth's tilt gives us our seasons.

We made it to the train station, and as we waited, members of the local model train club briefed us on Adelaide. They also proudly gave us a tour of their renovation of the local station. At 1100 we were in town and off on our separate adventures. Reg and Lynne were smart; they took the free tram to the beach, but Lynne said it was so hot, you could not walk on the sand. Lia, I'm sure went off to investigate something which I will find out about tomorrow.

I first went to the visitor center and then boldly set off to walk the streets in my usual fashion. Not today. The sun was blistering hot and it was not long before I retreated to the air conditioned South Australian Museum. Among the many absorbing displays was one featuring Australian Aboriginal Culture and the boomerang.

There are two types of boomerang, return and non-return. The return is smaller and used for sport and hunting small birds. If thrown properly, it will fly out as far as three hundred feet, curve to the left and return to the thrower. The non-return boomerang, used in war or for hunting large game, has less bend, is heavier, and can reach thirty-six inches in length. It can fatally injure an enemy or kill an animal up to five hundred feet away.

I needed to convert some dollars and this being Sunday, the only place where I could do that was the Sky City Casino. In addition, it was air conditioned and offered a three-dollar lunch. No pictures here, this is a casino. Actually the lunch cost four dollars with my loss of a dollar to the house.

Like Melbourne, Adelaide offers a free tourist bus around town and this too was air conditioned, so today we saw the city through glass rather then on foot. Adelaide was laid out in 1836 on a square grid pattern with airy parks similar to Savannah but without the moss-covered oak trees. The population is a million plus, and the town is set against a natural backdrop formed by the Adelaide Hills. On any day but today we would investigate further, but today I took the 1710-air-conditioned train back to the air-conditioned ship, ate ice cream, and made a pig of myself.

Mon, Feb 16   35° 14' 26"S
51 Mi. / 13728 Total Miles   137° 48' 12"E

At 0500 the stevedores, who had labored all night, finished their mysterious job of shuffling containers. Occasionally during the night we would hear what sounded like a crash of thunder when a container was lowered too quickly. All a normal part of the only reason we are here, to move containers.

At 0600 the ship, eager for a cool ocean breeze, left Adelaide under the command of a new, but familiar, master. Captain Ivan Bozanic, on the left with former Captain Alariky, was returning from leave and resuming his position as Master of the *Manet*.

Later, on the bridge, Captain Bozanic asked how I was enjoying the trip. In glowing terms I replied that so far the entire experience had been unique and enjoyable but I had two requests. Could we try the Filipino food that the crew eats, and could we have a tour of the engine room? He saw no problem with either, so we will see.

Not to dwell on the subject, but last Thursday we had a School Day about weights and measures and why we should adopt the metric system. Yesterday I had to convert Celsius degrees to Fahrenheit degrees and now I am on a soapbox about adopting Celsius. The background is simple. Mr. Fahrenheit devised a temperature scale where water freezes at 32° and boils at 212°. Mr. Celsius devised a temperature scale where water freezes at 0° and boils at 100°. Which scale is simpler to remember and makes more sense? Once again, the U.S. is the only country that uses Fahrenheit.

Yesterday the big issue was heat. Today it is wind. Having just returned from the bridge, I can tell you that the wind is blowing above gale force which is thirty-four knots. The *Manet* is pitching and rolling but I still feel comfortable. Lynne cannot say the same but her problem is not sea sickness. She was in her favorite spot, the bow, when she was suddenly drenched by a wave coming over the rail. Even that didn't wash away her smile.

This is the roughest weather of the trip and sometimes I wonder if those containers, which are stacked six high, are stable. This morning the deck crew was tightening the cross braces. However, they didn't seem worried and have probably seen weather much worse then this.

One final note for the day. This chapter is called *Southern Ocean*, but you won't find that name on many maps. It is a no-man's-land down here below Australia. Some maps call this area the Great Australian Bight, some call it the Southern Australian Basin, and some just lump it in with the Tasman Sea and the Indian Ocean. On the charts up in the bridge it is called the Southern Ocean. Today I would call it the Wild Ocean.

Tue, Feb 17   35° 29' 01"S
570 Mi. / 14298 Total Miles   127° 40' 28"E

Today we are going to jump ship. We are in the small white circle headed west toward Perth. Let's use this free day to get in our helicopter and visit Western Australia.

Western Australia, an area of 975,100 sq. mi, covers almost one-third of Australia and is one and one half times the size of Alaska. It has a population of fewer than two million, mostly settled around Perth, making  interior Western Australia one of the world's most sparsely settled regions. Even with a coastline of 7800 miles, most of this vast area is sandy and dry with little vegetation.

As we approach the southern coast in our helicopter, we are confronted with two-hundred foot limestone cliffs constantly pounded at their base by the Southern Ocean waves which we experienced yesterday. We fly right over these cliffs, but this coast is a graveyard for ships caught in storms and having no place to land.

As we set down, our wheels touch Nullarbor Plain, the world's largest single lump of limestone. One hundred thousand square miles and up to one thousand feet thick, this is an ancient seabed whose name, Nullarbor, means "no trees." Flat as a pancake, it contains Australia's longest straight stretch of highway (90 miles), and the world's longest straight stretch of railroad track (285 miles). The highway is occasionally used as a runway for Australia's famous Royal Flying Doctor Service. Fittingly, it is named Eyre Highway for Edward John Eyre, who in 1840, at age twenty-five, was the first European to cross this strange land.

Back in our helicopter, we fly north at jet speed seeking vegetation, but we could fly for a thousand miles over the Great Victorian Desert, Great Sandy, and Gibson deserts, seeing only cactuses and clumps of salt brush. If we slow down to helicopter speed, we may see a wombat, a camel, or a kangaroo; there is life down there, but to find human life and greenery we must find water.

The southwestern coast of Western Australia is home to a fertile region called Swanland. Here we find wheat, barley, oats, and orchards. Livestock is found on vast sheep and cattle ranches. Western Australia also leads the country in gold production and has large supplies of bauxite, nickel, and petroleum. We realize that Western Australia is so immense that we must be specific about what we are looking for. It is probably down there somewhere.

Time to head back to the *Manet* for dinner. Tomorrow evening we may have dinner in Perth, Capital of Western Australia.

Wed, Feb 18   35° 21′ 14″S
577 Mi. / 14875 Total Miles   117°25′ 08″E

We have grown so accustomed to it that its absence alarms us, but without it we wouldn't move. I could be talking about my heart, but you guessed it, I am talking about the ship's engine, the ship's heart. Today we have an invitation to enter that mysterious muscle that goes thump, thump, thump, all night long.

The chief engineer met me with a pair of gloves and a pair of ear muffs. The gloves I didn't need, the ear muffs, I wouldn't be without. The control room was modern, spotless, complicated, and quiet; a good place to get the facts.

For anyone interested, our power plant is a Hanjung Samsung Diesel, Type8S70. For the rest of us, it is one big mother.

If the engine is the heart of the ship, the control room is the heart of the engine. Filled with computers, gages, dials, and switches of every description, this is command control. From here the orders go out. Heat the heavy bunker fuel so that it will flow. Power the steam generator that provides heat for the ship and keeps the engine warm while in port. Run the four electric generators that supply power to the ship and 447 refrigerated containers. Take in sea water and under vacuum, condense it to fresh water for engine cooling and ship consumption. Direct the activities of a six-man staff. Maintain and be able to repair everything including a complete cylinder change, at sea, and yes, carry out orders from the bridge.

The engine has eight cylinders, each bigger than a Volkswagen Beetle. Those cylinders gobble up one hundred tons of fuel every day. Don't waste time figuring gallons or even barrels. Each cylinder requires one thousand pounds of bunker fuel every hour producing thirty-three thousand horsepower to drive the *Manet* at twenty-four knots.

From the control room we put on our ear muffs and step into a three-story high cavern which dwarfs our senses. Everything is supersized. The cylinder replacement strapped to the wall, the crank shaft bearing big enough to sit on, and the wrenches required for repairs, all are from another world, but even they are dwarfed by one thing, NOISE. A decibel meter would pop its fuse overwhelmed by the throbbing pound of thirty-three thousand horses. Each cylinder is a separate unit. No engine block would be large enough to hold these vibrating monsters. It is the same pulsating thump that I fall asleep to – six decks above.

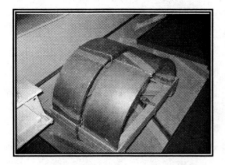 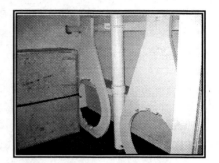

Unable to converse, the chief has told me that he will point out things now, and discuss them later in the quiet of his office. He leads me down flights of stairs to the aft of the ship. It is here that the torque from the pistons is transferred to the twenty-four foot, six blade propeller. That is done with a simple two foot diameter, solid steel shaft which directly connects the engine crankshaft to the propeller. There is no clutch and there is no transmission. When the captain wants to go forward, the engine which is always kept heated, is started. When he wants to go in reverse, the engine's rotation is reversed.

I stand there trying to comprehend that just beyond that steel hull, there is a giant propeller churning at eighty-eight revolutions per minute under twenty feet of water. I start to leave but the chief directs me to an even deeper chamber, still closer to the outside ocean. Moving the ship requires an engine, but that is useless without a rudder to steer the ship. He shows me how two giant hydraulic pistons move the rudder left or right in response to a helmsmen's delicate touch.

Back at his office he fills in the details of my questions. Finally I ask how many men are on the night shift? "None," he says. From the bridge, the officer on watch can monitor a few select gages and if problems occur, alarms go off. If the problem cannot be corrected and is serious, the chief engineer gets called out of bed. I leave, not wanting to know the possible ramifications.

Thu, Feb 19   32° 02' 46"S
248 Mi. / 15123 Total Miles   115° 44' 35"E

Perth has been called "the most isolated city in the world." It is closer to Jakarta, the capitol of Indonesia, then to Canberra, the capitol of Australia. John Glenn, the first American to orbit the earth, passed over Australia at night and against the blackness of the globe, he called Perth "the city of lights." From Perth, you could travel a thousand miles in any direction and not find a town large enough to require a traffic signal. Yet, it looks familiar. Have we traveled halfway around the world to find a city that looks like Dallas, Denver, or Detroit?

Perth   *Fremantle*

Today we visited Perth–Fremantle, and for this discussion I consider them as one. From the deck of our ship docked at Fremantle's port, you can see downtown Perth, and it is this small sliver of humanity on the west coast of Australia that we toured today.

At exactly midnight the *Manet* tied up at Fremantle's dock, just behind a sheep ship. More about sheep later. We went to bed hoping for an early morning trip into town. Up at 0600, Reg, Lynne, and I were ready to go right after breakfast, but where were the customs agents? Because of our limited time in port, this period of waiting is always frustrating.

Finally at 0930 we got permission to leave the ship and walked about a mile to the Fremantle train station. During our walk we were passed by at least a dozen tractor trailer trucks filled with sheep, four levels high, packed like sardines in a can. The smell when we returned to our ship in the afternoon, suggested that the procession of trucks had continued all day long. We found out later that those condemned sheep were headed to Jordan. We were headed to Perth.

A generic train took us to a generic station in a generic city. My first stop was the visitor center, to find a reason for coming this far, to find something I could see nowhere else. In response to that request, the young man behind the desk immediately suggested the Swan Bells.

Bells in their upright holding position

Swan Bell Tower

Swan Bells is one of the world's largest musical instruments. The three-year-old bell tower holds eighteen bells, some dating back to the fourteenth century. These Bells celebrated England's victory over the Spanish Armada in 1588. They welcomed Captain James Cook home in 1771, and they rejoiced at the victory of El Alamein in 1942. They were presented to Western Australia for its bicentennial, and today they rang for us, with live bell ringers swinging at the end of their ropes.

Certainly, the Swan Bells are unique, not to be found anywhere else in the world. Then there are the not unique, but ususal things like

miners striking gold and manikins selling apples.   Finally there is the franchise, the characteristic that, despite its remoteness, makes Perth exactly the same as any similar-sized city in the world. The Coca-Cola's, and MacDonald's, the KFC's, and Target's, (but no Wal-Mart); the names you see everywhere back home. So if Australians differ from Americans only when they say G'day Mate, does it make sense to travel and see the world? You are still with us on this odyssey, so I think I know your answer.

We started the day by looking for the unusual. After our return train ride from Perth, we found it in little Fremantle. The 20th century has touched Fremantle, but gently. Many of its historic buildings remain, having been turned into museums and art galleries. It was settled by the English in 1829 and could today serve as the movie set for a Victorian port of that era. Where else could you find a Cappuccino Strip or a Sardine Festival? Small towns and villages are often ideal places to find the unique. Plan to visit your Fremantle this weekend.

At the end of the day, Reg and Lynne found their reason for traveling the world. While at the Seaman's mission, waiting for a ride back to the ship, they met and renewed their acquaintance with a man who used to live just a short distance from their home in England. Small world.

With regret, we say G'day Mate to Australia and the Southern Ocean. We have visited four of the major cities here and seen much, but it is time to move on. When the *Manet* left port this evening, she turned north toward the Indian Ocean and new adventures.

CHAPTER SIX

Indian Ocean–East

⇒⇒⇒

Fri, Feb 20   32° 37' 36"S
175 Mi. / 15298 Total Miles   114° 12' 46"E

In any endeavor, reaching the mid point is significant. If you are able to reach the center mark, your chances of finishing are good. But where is the halfway point on this trip? There are at least four ways to measure.

1. Number of ports: We have visited or passed eleven of the twenty-one schedule ports.

2. Number of days: There are eighty days between January 12 and the now-estimated April 1 return to New York. We have just completed day forty.

3. Milage: CMA CGM estimates 32,421 miles for the voyage. This morning we passed forty-seven percent of that mileage.

4. Antipodes: Based on the following School Day, we have passed the halfway mark.

Antipodes

We are now at a point on the opposite side of the earth from where we began this adventure. If we bored a tunnel from here, through the earth's center and out the other side, the drill bit should pop out in Times Square. Any two locations, on opposite sides of the earth, are known as antipodes. Let's look at coordinates. Times Square is at latitude 40° 45' 30" N and longitude 073° 59' 09" W. Today we are at latitude 32° 37' 36" S and longitude 114° 12' 46" E (73 + 114 degrees equals 187). If we drill straight down from here, through the center of the earth and out the other side, our tunnel exit would not be at Times Square, but near Bermuda. Close enough for a passing grade.

Now suppose we chose to return home through this tunnel. What would we find and how would we feel? The entrance to our fictional tunnel would have to be watertight because the ocean beneath us is more then a mile deep. As we drop down through the ocean, then the ocean floor, we puncture the earth's crust consisting of twenty-five miles of solid granite and basalt. Then we pass through 1500 miles of viscous rock called the mantel. Temperatures and pressures are increasing now as we continue on through a liquid-iron-magnetic core which is also about 1500 miles thick. Finally we enter the 900-mile diameter, solid-iron crystal, that is the earth's center.

In reality we would have been cooked and crushed long ago, for here the temperature exceeds 10,000 degrees, and the pressure is millions of times greater then at the earth's surface. But if somehow we were able to survive, because of the earth's gravitational pull, we would be doomed to stay here at the earth's center forever. Because this is a fanciful journey, we will simply climb back through the crystal, core, mantle, and crust, to arrive in New York City just in time to catch the first act of a Broadway show.

Having traveled 8,000 miles through the center of our planet, you might ask; "Just how much does all this stuff weigh?" Since weight is relative to our location–I would weigh only 25 pounds on the moon–a better way to phrase the question is: What is the mass of the earth? The answer, which I am sure was on the tip of your tongue, is 6,500,000,000,000,000,000,000,000 tons. The more interesting question is, how did scientists come up with that figure? No, they did not use a scale, they simply used Newton's law of gravity. Any two masses have a gravitational attraction for one another. If we drop a known mass and measure the acceleration that earth's gravitational attraction applies to it, we can calculate the mass of the earth.

As for drilling a hole through the center of the earth, forget it. Man's deepest penetration into the earth to date is but a pinprick. In 1970 Russia began work on an exploratory drill hole. Thirteen years later when the project was cancelled for lack of funds, they had sunk a bit 40,225 feet, fewer then eight miles into the earth's crust.

Sat, Feb 21   22°14' 09"S
567 Mi. / 15865 Total Miles   110° 52' 39"E

Time again to review our journey. On January 12th, we left New York, sailed through the Panama Canal, across the Pacific, and down around the southern coast of Australia. Now we are headed north on the Indian Ocean to the Straits of Mallaca and Singapore. Then back across the Indian Ocean, through the Suez Canal to the Mediterranean Sea, up to the North Sea, and back across the Atlantic, to the good old U.S. of A. So we are halfway home, time to party!

And these men of the *Manet* know how to party. They do it with style. Not a lot of alcohol, but an abundance of food. At 1500 they started by roasting a suckling pig over a charcoal grill on the fantail of the ship.  For three hours the smoke and juices mixed with salt air so that by the time everyone gathered, the pig was cooked to perfection. Meanwhile Danny and his crew in the galley were preparing all the side dishes along with steaks, tuna, sausage, and more for those who don't like pork.

I don't normally eat a lot of meat but Danny, with knife in hand, said I must try it. I found it so good that I snuck back and cut off more.

Most of the crew members work on a nine-month contract which means three times around the world without seeing their families, and they work every day of the week. Gatherings like this are rare and it was evident that the crew needed and appreciated a break. Captain Bozanic officiated at the head of the table as both a man of authority and compassion. After finishing his meal, I noticed him make a point of moving among the men who were spread around the fantail.

After forty days on the *Manet*, I have become acquainted with many of these crew members to the degree that language will allow. It is tempting to romanticize about life at sea, but for the most part, they are hard-working family men who endure this life in order to provide a better life for their families back in the Philippines. I found pleasure in their pleasure.

Sun, Feb 22   14° 21' 57"S
579 Mi. / 16444 Total Miles   107° 50' 37"E

Last night at the party you informally met the ship's crew. I thought that today you might like an official introduction. Posted in the hallway of every deck level, is a complete roster of both the ship's personnel and passengers giving name, title, nationality, age, place of birth, and even passport number. The roster is not by rank so let's first take a look at the ship's order of seniority:

	Deck	Engine
Highest Officers:	Master	Chief Engineer
Senior Officers:	Chief Officer	2nd Engineer
Junior Officers:	2nd Officer	3rd Engineer
	3rd Officer	Asst. Electric
		Asst. Engineer
		4th Engineer
Subordinates:	1-Cook	
	1-Boatswain	
	10-Able Seaman	

And now it is my honor to present the crew of the *Manet.*

Title	Nationality	Year of birth
Master	Croatian	1960
Chief Officer	Croatian	67
2nd Officer	Filipino	58
3rd Officer	Filipino	66
Admin. Officer*	Filipino	58
Chief Engineer	Croatian	56
2nd Engineer	Croatian	54
3rd Engineer	Croatian	78
4th Engineer	Filipino	58
Electrician	Croatian	58
Boatswain	Filipino	52
Deck Fitter	Filipino	56
Able Seaman	Filipino	60
Able Seaman	Filipino	60
Able Seaman	Filipino	58
Engine Fitter	Filipino	55
Oiler	Filipino	65
Oiler	Filipino	55
Chief Cook	Filipino	54
2nd Cook	Filipino	54
Steward	Filipino	68
Engineer Cadet	Maltese	79

*previously Radio Officer

Let's hear a big round of applause!

CHAPTER SEVEN

Strait of Malacca
⇒ Singapore ⇒

Mon, Feb 23	06° 36' 36"S
569 Mi. / 17013 Total Miles	105° 00' 41"E

The party's over. Captain Bozanic has issued an *Anti-Piracy Watch and Attack Plan*. This is not a joke nor a drill.

For the next four days while we are in Indonesian waters the following rules will be enforced.

–Between sunset and sunrise, there will be a deck watch consisting of two men, one on port upper, one on starboard upper, with radios and lights. They should move irregularly about their posts and notify bridge of any suspicious craft or activity. Do not expose yourself to life danger.

–Outside cargo lights will remain on and fire hoses in ready.

–All outside doors will be locked between sunset and sunrise.

–Emergency signal will be seven short, followed by prolonged sounding of alarm.

–Bridge squad, Engine squad, Deck squad, report to assigned stations. Passengers remain locked in Owner's Cabin.

At 0900 we left the open waters of the Indian Ocean and squeezed through the narrow Sunda Strait, which separates Sumatra and Java. Past small islands, large chemical plants, and refineries, we wove our way through ships varying in size from freighters to tiny fishing boats. We are now sailing through the waters of the Republic of Indonesia, notorious for piracy. The following incidents were reported during one recent week on the Internet's *Weekly Piracy Report*.

19.11.2003 at 0330 LT in position 03:12n - 108 47.7e, 10nm off Pulau Subi Kecil. Indonesia
Duty officer on a tanker underway spotted an unlit craft on stbd beam at a distance of 5.0 nm. Speed 5.0kts. Craft increased speed to 16 kts and followed the tanker. Master took evasive action and craft moved away.

24.11.2003 at 0630 LT in position 01:21.1N - 117:01E, 14nm off Balikpapan, Indonesia.
Three pirates armed with guns and knives boarded a tanker via hawse pipe. They took hostage deck watch keeper at gun point. They stole ship's property and stores before escaping.

19.11.2003 at 2325 LT in position 01:17.9N - 104:06.1E, Eastern buoy, Singapore.
Seven pirates armed with long knives boarded a tanker underway and stole ship's cash and escaped.

Piracy prone areas and warnings
Indonesia - Anambas Island, Balikpapan, Bintan Island, Dumai, Gaspar, (Gelasa) Straits, Pulau Laut, Samarinda, Tanjong Priok.
Malacca straits - avoid anchoring along the Indonesia coast of the straits. Coast near Aceh is particularly risky for hijackings.

We are in an area of the world where piracy not only exists, but flourishes. At the same time, we are on a large, modern ship, knowledgeable of the danger, and prepared. Enough said about piracy.

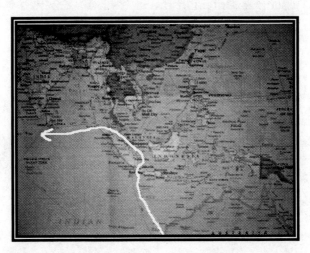

Southeast Asia: In my mind, it has always been as fuzzy as this picture. Let's try to sharpen it up a bit.

The prominent countries of Southeast Asia are not exactly household names but we should know them. Brunei, Cambodia, Indonesia, Laos, Malaysia, Philippines, Singapore, Thailand, and Vietnam. Tonight they surround us.

Generalizing is both difficult and dangerous but here goes. These countries are hot and humid because they are clustered around the equator. They have a diverse population, with densities often exceeding fifteen hundred per square mile. In population size, Indonesia ranks fourth behind China, India, and the U.S.. Islam, Hinduism, and Buddhism are the dominant religions. Millions are illiterate, yet Singapore ranks at the top on high school test scores.

I could continue to bore you with statistics and the importance of Southeast Asia, but one fact says it all. We are here, and I don't say that with a big ego. It would have been much shorter, easier, and safer for the *Manet* to go directly from Australia to the Suez Canal. We are here because Southeast Asia is important; tomorrow we will see why.

One quick item: This morning, as we passed through Sunda Strait, we also passed the six-square-mile island of Krakatau. Prior to the night of August 26, 1883, the size of Krakatau had been eighteen square miles. On that night a volcanic eruption and earthquake occurred, producing waves in excess of one hundred feet that traveled eight thousand miles, killing thousands. The explosion produced history's loudest noise; it was heard three thousand miles away. Good night.

Tue, Feb 24   00° 12′ 31″S
450 Mi. / 17463 Total Miles   106° 15′ 26″E

I must admit, this is being written on Wednesday because I was too tired to write last night. Please don't deduct points for lateness.

Yesterday was a day of contrast. The first half was typical. As we moved north in the Java Sea it was similar to the vast and lonely Indian Ocean, but around 1600 everything changed. With the first view, it was apparent why we had gone out of our way to come to Singapore.

We have visited ports that had two shore cranes and others that had none; Singapore has more than one hundred. They are so numerous that one picture could not begin to show the activity at this port. Captain Bozanic said that Rotterdam handles more container cargo but Singapore exceeds all ports in ship traffic. Without doubt, we have seen more ships this afternoon than on the entire trip to date.

The Republic of Singapore is an independent city-state. It consists of one main island, and numerous small adjacent islands, totaling less than two hundred-fifty square miles. It is connected to the country of Malaysia by a causeway. Its population is multiracial and estimated at three million. Seventy-eight percent are Chinese but the official language is English.

In the 1820's, Sir Thomas Stamford Raffles began transforming a few small fishing villages into a British trading post. Over the next one hundred years, this free-trade port, located between the South China Sea and Indian Ocean, became Southeast Asia's most important seaport, and today its  citizens enjoy one of the world's highest standards of living.

Loading and unloading goes on twenty-four hours a day at this port and despite the late hour we were anxious to jump ship and see Singapore. By 1930, with passports and paperwork, Reg, Lynne, and I were at the port gate—but that's as far as we got. Gate Security said we needed another stamp on our passport besides the one Customs had already put there.

At times like this it's helpful to have experienced travelers for companions. I have mentioned that Reg has a quick tongue. He can also be tactfully assertive if necessary, a lethal combination. Within a half hour he had the captain call the port agent, who met us at the gate. This time Security was apologetic and waved us through. Meanwhile Lynne, who seems to thrive on uncertainty, was enjoying the whole affair. Her infectious excitement turned a pain into a sparkling memory. Once through the gate we parted, chuckling.

The hour was late and it was a strange city, but Criss had mentioned Tanjong Pagar, a street which leads away from the port area. I found it, and followed it for a mile or two, ending up in Chinatown. Needing neither a blouse nor a fish head dinner, I decided

 to call Marise and then call it an evening. Back on the *Manet*, I scanned the map given by a now helpful security guard, and got things ready for an early start tomorrow morning.

Wed, Feb 25   01° 15' 54"N
195 Mi. / 17658 Total Miles   103° 50' 32"E

It's 0500, still dark out, but those cranes have been loading all night, and shore leave expires at 1200; let's go. But before we head out, take a quick look at our latitude. It has switched from S to N, meaning that we crossed the equator and are now back in the northern hemisphere. This trip is moving on and so are we–off to Singapore.

The following note is stamped on our shore leave pass: *Warning, death for drug traffickers under Singapore law.* Singapore has tough laws with severe penalties, jaywalking–$50, smoking in public places–$500, littering–up to $1000.

They claim title to the safest large city in the world. We feel secure walking the dark, almost deserted streets. An old woman sweeping last night's leaves off the sidewalk with her corn broom says good morning. A few joggers and exercisers are out seeking eternal life in the cool morning air. How fortunate we are to witness and not intrude.

Within moments it seems, we see the city come alive. Subway trains empty their loads from suburbia onto city sidewalks and return for more. Bridges crossing the Singapore River clog with Mercedes, each carrying one passenger to his oval office. Each, in their own world, pauses briefly at the news stand to buy into world events. Again we marvel at our good fortune to be able to witness and not participate.

 We are free to meditate in the parks, stroll the river walk a l o n g Singapore  River, investigate the downtown business district, or shop along world-famous Orchard Road, where Gucci is just another handbag.

We do all these things but time runs out. Much as we would like to view the city from a Chinese water taxi, we must return to our own water taxi, the *Manet*.

Singapore is a city of opulence, status, luxury, and power. It is not my city. I do not begrudge them their world of wealth, but prefer a world of simplicity. I seek the experience of Singapore, not the trappings. My Mercedes is a pair of walking shoes; my oval office is the world.

The best things in life are not things.

Thu, Feb 26   03° 45' 38"N

325 Mi. / 17983 Total Miles   099° 51' 01"E

At 1730 yesterday our pilot disembarked, and Singapore faded into its perpetual tropical haze. We are again headed north in the Strait of Malacca, a nautical highway for everything from ocean ships to sampans. Let me describe the bizarre view from my porthole at 0200 last night.

As the window swung open, the air conditioning was swept aside and I was bathed in a rush of damp warm air. A few of the brightest stars were visible, but mist obscured most, and every few moments a flash of heat lightening would bring life to the fog. Strung out on both sides of us marched a parade of silent, ghostly ships, lights ablaze to thwart pirates, all racing at the same tempo to clear this notorious area. A surreal sight indeed.

On my daily trip to the bow I was again stirred by another sight. We have just passed Kuala Lumpur, capital city of Malaysia, and home to Petronas Towers, the world's tallest building. These are not third world people, yet ten miles off their shore the sea is a garbage dump. Everything from flotsam to florescent lights. Shame.

Enough preaching from me, time for a School Day.

Global Weather

Every evening we check our local weather on the TV news. Occasionally we switch to the Weather Channel and view the national weather, but rarely do we even think about global weather. Local weather is just that, local. It is effected by terrain, seasons, cities, and other variables. To nullify these local variables we have to view the planet from afar, let's say the moon. Do you remember that spectacular picture taken by the Apollo astronauts showing Earth rising over Moon's horizon? That is our perspective. From that distance, by looking at the clouds, we can see global wind patterns that are, in part, responsible for our local weather. As we travel the globe, these wind patterns change. Let's take a look.

Because the sun's rays are most direct here at the equator, the air within 10 degrees latitude either side of the equator is usually hot and humid. Hot air rises because it is less dense, and therefore lighter then cooler air. This expanded air rises and travels north from the equator at an elevation of about four miles. At this elevation the air slowly cools, becomes heavy, and sinks back down to earth somewhere around 30° N, which just happens to be the latitude of Jacksonville, Florida. So we have high pressure at 30° and low pressure at the equator, forcing the surface winds to travel south again to complete the circle.

Now, superimpose the earth's rotation on these southerly surface winds and they are redirected to the southwest. These are the same dependable winds that Columbus and other early traders used to sail from Europe to the New World, hence the name Trade Winds.

At latitudes where air is sinking or rising, namely the equator, 30°N, 60°N, and 90°N the surface winds are relatively light, rendering poor sailing conditions. At the equator these quiet wind conditions are called the Doldrums; at 30°N, they are called the Horse Latitudes because becalmed sailors threw their animals overboard when feed ran out.

The process just described which occurs between 0° and 30° is referred to as a closed thermal cell and is repeated twice again as we move northward toward the pole. At 60° N, the approximate latitude of Anchorage, Alaska, relatively warm air is rising causing low pressure at the surface and at the North Pole, 90° N, cold air is sinking resulting in high pressure. Between 30° and 60° N latitudes, where most of the United States lies, the prevailing winds are to the east, which is opposite of the Trade Winds between 0° and 30° N.

Each fall we witness the power of these thermal cells. A small weather disturbance is born off the coast of Africa. The Trade Winds push it westward across the Atlantic for days as it increases in strength to hurricane status. At some point, usually around the Gulf of Mexico, it swings northward crossing the 30th parallel. It then reverses course and turns northeast being caught up in the westerly winds.

Of course the mirror image of these three thermal cells also exists in the Southern Hemisphere creating their own weather patterns, but we seldom hear about all this action because we are watching our local TV station. To see the pattern of global winds, we need more weather reports from the moon.

Fri, Feb 27   05° 59′ 08″N
564 Mi. / 17547 Total Miles   091° 57′ 35″E

We have cleared the Strait of Malacca and the pirate alert has been lifted. Overnight on our starboard side, we passed the coasts of Thailand and Burma, now called Myanmar. Based on this morning's latitude and longitude readings, if you were to dive off the ship and swim directly north for seven hundred miles through the Bay of Bengal, you would arrive on the beach of Bangladesh. But if you chose not to get wet, stay on board and we will discuss some housekeeping items.

Item: The ship's current is 220 volts at 50 cycles. Depending on your country of origin, you will need an adapter to fit the ship's socket and a converter to change the voltage. Appliances in the U.S. run on 110 volts, 60 cycles. You will need an adapter which goes from the ship's two round prongs to your appliance's two flat prongs. You will also need a converter to reduce the voltage from 220 to 110. Two caveats: one, except for extremely sensitive appliances, cycles per second does not matter and two, computers and some battery chargers have converters built in, but you still need an adapter; check the power label. Both units are available at Radio Shack for under $20.

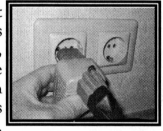

Item: I am not qualified to write on this item, but that hasn't stopped me yet. E-mail is possible and Lia sends it all the time using the ship's computer in the Administrative Office. Carl and Pancha wrote their messages in their cabin to a floppy disk, then Danny sent them via the ship's computer. The ship's e-mail address is long and complicated and some of their messages were rejected by the recipients junk mail screen. Telephone calls are possible both in and out, but expensive. One thing you can count on, every ship's facilities and policies will be different. If communication is important, check in advance.

Item: Money. You need none on board except for purchases from the slop chest. Caveat: I understand some freighters have cash bars; check ahead if booze is important. We all have our personnel ways for handling money for shore purchases and tips. ATM's supplying local cash are everywhere, as are official money changers and banks. Still, be safe and carry a supply of small denomination U.S. currency. Tip: Purchase a supply of odd-color plastic ties (for wrapping electrical wires) at a hardware store. Use them for securing your luggage zippers. They won't stop a thief, but if the tie is cut, at least you'll know he's been there.

Item: Your cabin window may be blocked depending on how high containers are stacked. Mine has been blocked for about half the trip. I very seldom open it because

Blocked   Unblocked

of heat and noise. Container ships have a constant background noise from the electric coolers on the containers. Of course if you have a side window, no problem.

Item: Water is both plentiful and potable. I constantly replenish a water bottle from my bathroom faucet with no health problems and there is always a pitcher of ice water on the dining table. Ice, if desired, is available from a machine on B Deck. Showers provide unlimited hot water–don't tell the chief engineer I said that.

I hope your accommodations are comfortable because we won't be getting off this ship for nine or possibly twelve days. We are now back in the Indian Ocean on a due west course headed for the Red Sea and Suez Canal. The latest schedule has us in Jeddah, Saudi Arabia on March 3rd but the Saudis prohibit disembarkation, even to touch their soil. The next possible stop is in Egypt on March 7th for only fifteen hours. Malta, on March 10th is our next definite shore leave port.

CHAPTER EIGHT

Indian Ocean–West
⇒⇒⇒

Sat, Feb 28   05° 51′ 41″N
603 Mi. / 18150 Total Miles   083° 10′ 52″E

If we are going to be at sea for ten days, I think it only prudent that I check the food supply. Danny, the cook, assures me that I needn't worry but I wanted to see for myself, so he promised to show me everything except where the ice cream is hidden. Smart man.

Starting at 0400 to bake the daily bread and rolls, Danny and his part-time assistant, Oscar, must prepare three meals a day for crew and passengers (28 people), mostly from scratch, and to suit western, Croatian, and Filipino tastes. He performs this miracle seven days a week using his personal cookbook. He is also responsible for ordering, receiving, and accounting for all provisions, cleanliness of the galley, even preparing and typing the daily menu.

Somehow he found time to show us around his kingdom which has two castles, the galley, and the freezers. His kitchen is just like yours and mine, only supersized. He measures his eggs not by the dozen, but by the case, and remember, he can't hop in the car and zip down to the corner market for an extra pound of butter. He stocks up every three weeks or so, requiring lots of storage space, most of it refrigerated.

There are four walk-in freezers, each held at a different temperature appropriate for meat, fish, dairy, and produce. Before entering we must put on a winter coat and go down a flight of stairs to A Deck, meaning everything must be hauled up a flight of stairs to the galley. The temperature gages were all in Celsius, but in Fahrenheit they ranged from produce at 40° to meat at 0°.

All fears of starvation were allayed when I saw the cases of cereal and mountains of meat. Each day Danny must gather in advance, tomorrow's food, and let it thaw at the proper rate. That in itself is a science. Can you imagine the plight of this ship if its crew were stricken with food poisoning?

In one freezer hung the lamb, ready to be roasted at the next ship's party. In another freezer sat the jam waiting to be spread on our morning toast. There were bags of flour and sacks of rice, both needing refrigeration to prevent insect infestation. There were cartons of milk and cases of juice, all with their expiration dates clearly recorded. In the produce freezer resided the carrots, cucumbers, potatoes, and papayas. Anything and everything needed for the next few weeks –except the bananas. Bananas are fussy; keep them too cool and they stay green, keep them too warm and they turn brown. Keep them in Danny's secret climate, and they stay a golden yellow.

True to his word, Danny has ample stores for our Indian Ocean voyage and also true to his word, I never saw the ice cream.

Sun, Feb 29   07° 20' 35"N
574 Mi. / 18724 Total Miles   074° 56' 43"E

We have arrived at a very interesting intersection on this road around the world, and since we will pass this way only once in a lifetime, it might be wise to stop and look around. For the next three days we will maintain a 285° heading while crossing the Arabian Sea, part of the Indian Ocean. Anytime during this transit, if we look to the east, we see India, to the north we see the middle east, and to the west, we see Africa. Surely a good place to pause and learn.

Before you say boring, boring, consider this; next time your computer crashes and you call tech support you will probably be talking to someone halfway around the world in India. Or, sad to say, if you are approaching military age, you might want to know a little about the middle east before signing up.
Glance at your finger. The gold in that ring may have been mined in Africa. Or maybe your ancestors came from any one of these areas. So stay with us, it's a long swim to shore.

Yesterday, around 1400, we passed the southern tip of Sri Lanka, clearly seeing its tall white light house that marked our entrance to the Arabian Sea. Sri Lanka, about the size of West Virginia, lies off the coast of India. The southern half is a popular European vacation spot with exclusive resorts and palm-lined beaches. Their main export is the highly prized Sri Lankan tea, but unfortunately we know the country best for its ongoing war.

Since 1960, the eight percent Muslim minority in the north has sought a separate nation. In 1983 civil war broke out between the government and the rebel Liberation Tigers, a group that claims to represent the Muslim Tamil minority. There have been on and off peace talks and India has occasionally intervened on the side of Sri Lanka, but the conflict sporadically continues to this day with no end in sight.

India, at one million square miles, is the world's seventh largest country. Shaped like a triangle, its northern boundary is the Himalayas, containing the world's highest mountains. Having recently passed the one billion population mark, it is expected to surpass China within a decade as the world's most populous country.

A land of many cultures, religion plays an important role with Hinduism being the religion of eighty percent, followed by Muslims, Christians, Sikhs, and Buddhists. More than fifteen major languages are spoken in thousands of local dialects.

Before British supremacy in the 1700's, India was a loose conglomerate of empires and kingdoms. As we have seen in other countries, the British Empire did much to develop these countries, not for benevolent reasons mind you, but for domination, trade, and exploitation. Nevertheless, under British rule and indirectly the English East India Company, India flourished.

Again, as we have seen, the cry for independence from England continued to grow. Violence and strikes were an ongoing problem, not only between England and India but between Hindu and Muslim. During this period, an Indian lawyer named Mahatma Gandhi gained prominence as a political figure with a different philosophy. He espoused nonviolence, civil disobedience, and fasting–new weapons in the war for independence. He won worldwide support and is given most of the credit for England's capitulation.

Finally, in 1947 India won its self-determination from England and Pakistan was split off as a separate, primarily Muslim, country. India and Pakistan both still claim Kashmir and other border territories. Since each country has nuclear weapons, these disagreements could affect the world.

Today India, while not a superpower, is a prominent world leader. It is a democratic country with voting rights for all. The United States is India's largest trading partner from whom we import, among other things, textiles, chemicals, and electronics.

Education is selective. Because of the large population, many are illiterate, but those that receive an education receive a good one. Visit Silicon Valley or better yet, go to your local hospital. When you wake up after your operation, chances are good that you will see an Indian face smiling down at you.

Mon, Mar 1   09° 37′ 39″N
596 Mi. / 19320 Total Miles   066° 31′ 55″E

   Surprise! Last night Captain Bozanic declared another party.
Now aren't you glad you stayed on board for the India lecture. This
time it was BYOB. For you tea drinkers, that's Bring Your Own Booze.
I ordered a case of beer and was pleased to see it labeled "passenger/
American." I do my part to spread good will.

   No barbequed pig this time. The captain described it as a
picnic. Weather and sea conditions limit his discretion to declare a
party. They probably won't have another until sometime after Panama,
and we won't be there—unless you care to go around again? The chap
in the photo will win the whole bottle if he can drink wine from both
glasses without using his hands or setting one down.

   Now, back to our intersection. Yesterday we turned east and
visited India. Today, a turn to the west takes us to Africa, but where
does one begin to explore Africa? I suggest the beginning, the very
beginning!

   Human life began in Africa more than five million years ago,
which means that if we go back far enough, our ancestors came from
Africa. More than five thousand years ago, Africa was home to one of
the world's first great civilizations, the Egyptian empire.

   After Asia, Africa is the second largest of the earth's seven
continents. It comprises about twenty-two percent of the world's land
area and contains twelve percent of the world's population. The
world's largest desert divides the continent. The Sahara runs east-west
from the Atlantic to the Red Sea, and beyond to Iraq. It seems bizarre,
but in a few days we will be passing through the Sahara Desert on a
ship.

North of the Sahara the countries of Egypt, Libya, Algeria, and Morocco tend to be more developed than those to the south. It is here that we not only find the world's largest desert, but ironically, the world's longest river, the 4145 mile-long Nile. This region, known as North Africa is united by the Arabic language and the religion of Islam, both merged in the Koran, the sacred scripture of Islam.

South of the Sahara we find Negroid peoples who make up seventy percent of Africa's population. The basic social unit of this Negroid group is the extended family which is often linked to a larger social group or clan.

As early as 1500, Portugese expeditions, followed by English, French, and Dutch traders began disrupting social patterns that had existed for centuries. This was followed by four centuries of slave trade when millions of African natives were captured, mostly by other Africans, traded for goods and weapons, then sent as slaves to countries around the world. Near the end of the eighteenth century, sentiment in Great Britain turned against slave trading and civil war in the United States ended slavery, essentially ending this barbaric practice.

By the mid 1800's Britain, France, Germany, and other European countries established colonies in Africa. Without consultation with, or consent from the citizens, they carved out and claimed territories as their protectorates. This practice was resisted by the local rulers but often welcomed by the oppressed. It also led to competition and conflicts between the occupying powers.

After World War I, exploitation of Africa tapered to some degree with greater emphasis placed on social welfare. In some cases colonies were given the power to self govern but the governing party was usually the white settlers. Africans were not permitted to participate or vote. Resistance to colonization continued but often strayed from its goal of independence due to internal conflicts among the Africans.

Following World War II, countries achieved independence at a faster rate. In 1960 alone, seventeen African countries were born and by 1980 most of Africa had achieved self-rule. Yet conflict continues.

Today, the African continent encompasses more than fifty sovereign nations. Some are peaceful and prosperous, unfortunately, in many, poverty and strife rule with little sign of resolution.

Tue, Mar 2   11° 48′ 10″N
584 Mi. / 19904 Total Miles   058° 27′ 59″E

Before class today let's hit a few of the morning highlights. Since Carl left the ship in Auckland, I have been going to the bridge before breakfast to chart our location and chat with the first mate. This morning he was complaining about paperwork, feeling that he is no longer a seaman but rather a secretary, especially with all the new security regulations.

I mentioned this at the breakfast table and Reg began complaining about passport photos. Before leaving England, he and Lynne had to pay an extra twenty-five quid for odd-sized passport photos required only by the U.S. It seems that everyone is in a bad mood this morning. The only person smiling is Criss as he holds his grouchy watermelon.

The third and final leg of our intersection points north and it may be the most difficult to understand. Civilization began here, but today people are blowing themselves up attempting to kill it. From the Indian Ocean we pass through the Arabian Sea and enter the Persian Gulf. To our right lay the countries of Pakistan, Afghanistan, Iran, Iraq, and Kuwait. Anyone who has not heard these names in the past decade has been at sea too long. These countries, along with others that we will view from the Red Sea, are a part of Asia called the Middle East. War and violence seem synonymous with the Middle East.

Thirty-five hundred years before Christ, the Sumerian civilization, considered by some historians to be the first civilization, lived in a land called Mesopotamia between the Tigris and Euphrates Rivers, the "cradle of civilization." They gave birth to cities, devised a system of writing, and were the people who actually invented the wheel. Today the Tigris River runs right through downtown Baghdad, so you see, we are in a land with a long history of both creativity and chaos.

In time the Sumerians were conquered by the Babylonians who were in turn overthrown by the Assyrians who were replaced by the Persian Empire, and on and on it went.

As all this was going on, there existed in the background, a small group called Hebrews whose name means "those who pass from place to place." At different times they were subjects in lands ruled by others, slaves to the Egyptians, or wandering nomads. They traced their roots back to Abraham who lived near the Tigris River between 2000 and 1500 BC.

Interestingly, three of the world's great religions, Christianity, Judaism, and Islam claim Abraham as a patriarch. After the birth of Christ, some Hebrews converted to Christianity but many maintained their Jewish faith and during the next two millennia carried it to all parts of the world. In 1948 after World War II, land was set aside in the Middle East for the Jewish State of Israel.

Going back to the sixth century, Muhammad was born in Mecca, and as a young man he experienced a vision from the archangel Gabriel who proclaimed him a prophet of God. From these revelations he wrote the Koran which today is the Holy Book of the Muslim faith. It is necessary to consider these religions which we skimmed over today in order to understand the conflicts that continue in this part of the world.

By 1500 AD, the once unified Islamic world had begun to divide into separate kingdoms. The Ottoman Empire ruled lands around the entire eastern half of the Mediterranean. However, their rule was exercised through local tribes, and as time passed these tribes strengthened into self-regulating autonomies, often with differing interpretations of Islam.

Combine this mix with intervention and colonialism from the U.S. and European powers and you have a problem. Then stir in two world wars with their alliances and settlements and you have a dilemma. Add the establishment of a Jewish state in Palestine displacing Arabs who claim it as their home, and you have a quandary. Pour in the discovery of oil and sprinkle the entire boiling pot with a high rate of unemployment and despair and you run out of adjectives and solutions.

Needless to say, this is an area of our world that defies a peaceful settlement of its problems. Historic hatreds are numerous and are accepted as a normal way of life. Nevertheless, there is no other reasonable option then continued diplomacy toward a resolution.

Wed, Mar 3   12° 46' 19"N
581 Mi. / 20485 Total Miles   049° 54' 37"E

    This will be our last day on the Indian Ocean. Last night we saw land off the port side which was the African country of Somalia, another country besieged by civil war and anarchy. Today we are passing through the Gulf of Aden and tonight we will enter the Red Sea. This is the route taken by all ships carrying cargo between Europe and Asia so we should see a lot of shipping activity during the next few days.

    Last night I was able to get a picture of our three senior officers. Take a look at that, then we will go on to a School Day, then a new chapter.

Chief Officer   *Captain*   *Chief Engineer*

Global Shipping

    For two months we have been witnesses to an industry that affects us all but usually goes completely unnoticed. The shipping industry transports ninety percent of the world's trade which means that if you look around the room you are sitting in, virtually everything that came from outside the United States crossed the ocean at one time or another in a container similar to the ones we are carrying on this ship. Your $500 TV sitting in the corner cost $25.30 to ship and the $1.00 can of imported beer in your hand paid 4.2 cents for the boat ride. Put all these revenues together and the World Bank estimates that international shipping annually contributes three hundred billion dollars to the world economy.

Trade is as old as civilization itself, making shipping the first global industry. Today there are more than fifty thousand cargo carrying ships which, in aggregate, could carry approximately 530,000,000 tons.

TYPE	NUMBER OF SHIPS
General cargo	20,711
Tanker	10,923
Bulk Carrier	5,850
Passenger	2,719
Container	2,579
Other	2,534

To the outsider the shipping industry looks like a tangled web. The cost of a modern cargo ship easily exceeds one hundred million dollars and it may be owned by one company, leased by another, managed by a third, and staffed by an international crew. It may fly the flag of any country but the most popular flags are:

COUNTRY	GROSS TONNAGE
Panama	112,106,000
Liberia	49,970,000
The Bahamas	30,787,000
Malta	25,949,000
Greece	25,902,000

The United States comes in eighth with 21 million tons.

These fifty thousand ships are manned by 400,000 officers and 825,000 other ratings for an average of twenty-five crew members per ship. Having said that we should note that passenger ships, which are included in this calculation, have a much larger staff then cargo ships.

Finally, let us look at shipping as compared to other modes of cargo transport in relation to the environment. Comparison is both difficult and questionable, but due to the enormous tonnage carried by one ship the energy efficiency of shipping clearly exceeds that of highway and rail.

CHAPTER NINE

Red Sea
⇒ Jeddah ⇒ Suez Canal ⇒ Damietta ⇒

Thu, Mar 4   14°29′ 41″N
510 Mi. / 20995 Total Miles   042° 31′25″E

First, let us establish that the Red Sea is not red, despite the demands of one of the first mate's former passengers. He scornfully related the account at our morning meeting.

He has had an eventful morning and can be forgiven for being on edge. About 0500 I suddenly awoke to find the ship leaning precariously. It was an anxious moment, hearing things begin to slide across the floor and items fall out of the medicine chest. Your sense of balance tells you that we had better not tip any further or we won't be returning upright. Grasping the window frame, I got to the porthole just in time to see lights sliding by on our starboard side. The *Manet* seemed to sense her predicament and struggled to regain equilibrium. Slowly at first, but with increasing confidence, she shifted her center of gravity back to its rightful place. Regaining her poise, we sailed on.

My morning question about the episode brought little response at first, but in time he related that a fishing boat had suddenly moved across his path, forcing the maneuver. He implied that it was nothing–nothing for him maybe. Under normal conditions at sea, the ship is on auto pilot, but for emergency maneuvers the officer on watch navigates by experience with one eye on the clinometer. He excused the fisherman as possibly being blinded by their own work lights but then said that if a collision had occurred, it would have produced a slight thud, a scratch in the *Manet's* paint and worst of all, a casualty report.

Today we are well into the Red Sea which separates northeastern Africa from the Arabian peninsula. Yemen is on our starboard side and Eritrea on our port side but all we see is an  occasional uninhabited island. Combined with the Suez Canal, which we will pass through on Sunday, these two waterways will take us to the Mediterranean Sea and Europe. An odd shaped body of water, the Red Sea is fourteen hundred miles long and two hundred miles wide.

Without getting into Plate Tectonics, which deals with movement of the earth's crust, we can say that the Red Sea was formed twenty million years ago when the Arabian Peninsula split away from Africa.

Tomorrow the first mate will again be busy at 0500. That is when we pick up a pilot for the port city of Jeddah, Saudi Arabia. Weeks ago we had been told that we would not be able to get off the ship at Jeddah and yesterday this notice went up. It not only warned us about having liquor and pornography, but Lynne was told to get rid of a fashion magazine. Both Lynne and Lia, the only women on board, have been told that they must wear clothing that covers their arms and legs. At the gym/library, I noted that everything had been removed from the book shelves, placed in bags and boxes and readied for storage while in Jeddah. Tomorrow should prove to be an interesting day.

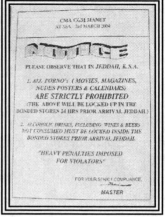

Fri, Mar 5   21°26' 58"N
532 Mi. / 21527 Total Miles   039° 01' 19"E

One of the few pleasures of coming to Jeddah is consuming and disposing of all the open bottles of wine the night before we arrive. I did my part to keep us out of trouble.

We had been told stories about Jeddah, but I wanted to view it with an open mind. After docking at 0830, I went up on the monkey deck with a pair of field glasses. Above me on the mast flew the green Saudi Flag with the Arabic inscription, "There is no God But Allah, and Muhammad is Allah's Prophet." Under the inscription lies a sword. Below me walked an armed guard. During the day the gangplank remained up, lowered only for stevedores and a few officials and then only with the guard nearby. The welcome mat was nowhere to be seen.

Through my binoculars I saw a nondescript city of two million spread out in the desert haze. Almost all buildings were white, most lower than five stories with a few twenty-story buildings sprinkled about. One ultra modern mosque stood out and I could pick out several others by spotting the tall tower, or minaret, where prayers are given. One landmark that stood out above all others was a tower at the  harbor entrance. The captain later said that it was a combination port headquarters and water tower.

If my binoculars had been stronger, I would have seen a country slightly larger than Alaska. Most of its people live in large cities such as Riyadh, the capital; or Mecca, Islam's most holy city; birthplace of Muhammad. It is a monarchy with the King selected for life from the Royal Family and an economy based primarily on oil. It is ironic that here we have one of the richest countries in the world, and just two hundred miles directly across the Red Sea lies the country of Sudan, one of the world's poorest. Oil makes a big difference.

My viewing was interrupted when Criss came to tell me that Customs wanted to see me. In the conference room the captain introduced me to a uniformed official asking that I show the officer my room. We shook hands, and I complied. He entered my room, briefly glanced around, opened the refrigerator, then thanked me and left. I later found that he had followed a similar scenario with the other passengers. Should I have acquiesced to his demands to search my private room? It would make a good high school debate.

A more interesting question is, why is Saudi Arabia closed to foreigners? We have visited a dozen ports and while we never saw a red carpet laid out, we also never saw an armed guard. If allowed to go into town, I might have met someone, had a friendly chat, and come away with a much different perception and description of Saudi Arabia. Instead, I was pleased when the *Manet* pulled in her lines and slipped away from the pier.

Tonight we are back on the Red Sea, four weeks from America, which is looking better all the time.

Sat, Mar 6   25° 49' 56"N
377 Mi. / 21904 Total Miles   035° 28' 58"E

Tonight we drift at anchor for the first time since waiting to enter the Panama Canal. We wait here because tomorrow we pass through another canal, the Suez. There will be no locks this time but we can still expect an exciting day.

Another major change today. It has turned cold. For one of the few times since Savannah, I have put on a pair of long pants. A trip out on deck would require a sweatshirt or jacket.

Our morning was warm and sunny as we continued north in the Red Sea. We crossed the Tropic of Cancer but no one paid any attention, and we won't either. Just after lunch the wind picked up and before long it was blowing at gale force. Fortunately it was blowing directly at us so we didn't rock much but poor *Manet* took a pounding.

At times spray would reach the bridge, making it difficult to get a good picture without getting the camera wet. Captain Bozanic called it a desert wind saying that at times it can reach hurricane force. Today's top winds were about fifty knots but tonight, except for the temperature, the weather has returned to normal. Yesterday the ladies had to cover their legs with long pants for Muslim tradition. Today we all wear pants for comfort.

As we continued north, we began to see oil rigs, both on land and in the water, each with their little burn-off flame wiped by the wind. Most were small and probably unmanned but occasionally we would pass one with a large platform capable of maintaining a support crew.

We are now in the Gulf of Suez at the northern end of the Red Sea. Egypt surrounds us on both shores. This country with sixty-five million people is half the size of Alaska and Cairo is its capitol. Like Saudi Arabia, Egypt also exports oil but has smaller reserves. Their history goes back to 3000 BC with the Egyptian Empire at its height around 1400 BC. In 332 BC, Egypt fell to Alexander the Great who founded Alexandria. One thousand years later Arabs, who introduced Islam, conquered Egypt. Modern Egypt won independence from Great Britain in 1922.

It is dark now but this afternoon as the Red Sea narrowed, all we saw on both shores was desert sprinkled with oil wells. We saw no towns, but there was something of much greater interest out there.

The shore to our east is the Sinai Peninsula and somewhere over there is Mount Sinai. If you know your Old Testament, you know that Mount Sinai was where Moses went to receive the Ten Commandments. He then went on to part the Red Sea and lead the Jews out of Egyptian bondage to the promised land. Tonight we drift and continue to wait in this land of violence for mankind to honor the sixth commandment, thou shall not commit murder.

Sun, Mar 7   29° 54′ 06″N
334 Mi. / 22238 Total Miles   032° 31′ 11″E

Chalk up another big milestone on our round the world adventure. Today we passed through the Suez Canal and tonight I am bushed. All day long I have been standing out on deck in bitter cold wind, trying to get a good picture of the canal. Sorry, this is the best I could do for you, and here is why.

The Suez Canal is nothing but a big ditch. I don't mean that it is not important or interesting, I mean that I simply don't know how to photograph a big ditch. Here are the facts.

The Suez Canal is one hundred-twenty miles long. It is two hundred feet wide and fifty feet deep, large enough for a 150,000 ton ship. It was opened in 1869 and controlled by the British and French until 1956 when Egypt nationalized it. It has been closed twice, both times due to ships being sunk during wartime.

When I went to the bridge at 0600, the captain and first mate were having morning coffee. While waiting for the pilot, they confided that this is known as Marlboro Country. Everyone wants a "gift" of cigarettes before they will go to work. Depending on rank, they are given a pack or a carton.

As the sun came up I could see that we were surrounded by ships that had anchored last night. The canal is not wide enough for ships to pass, mandating convoys in each direction. We were scheduled to be number eleven in a convoy of sixteen ships.

At 0700 a large navy ship, too far off to tell what country, began to move. For the next hour we waited as one by one the parade of goliaths fell into place and moved out, each piloted by an Egyptian officer, and each spaced about a half mile apart. Finally the *Manet* slipped into eleventh position and we were off.

I could not help but juxtapose these pictures. The sword is as tall as the Statue of Liberty but dwarfed by her message. "*Give me your tired, your poor, your huddled masses, yearning to breath free.*"

For the next ten hours we cruised through the canal at half speed, always keeping the half-mile separation. One thing quickly became apparent. On the starboard side lies the Sinai Peninsula which was once captured by Israel during the Six Day War, but later returned to Egypt during peace talks. Today it remains desert interrupted only by an occasional Egyptian Military guard house. On the port side, which was always Egyptian, the land is developed.

Every ten miles or so on the port side there were small towns usually having some light industry. At one point, along a beach, I saw some rather expensive looking homes, but for the most part, these people are poor. Small cultivated areas and a few palm trees were scattered along the banks but little else. The canal was straight for long stretches and included two natural lakes where ships could pass. At one of these lakes we passed a large warship named the Charles de Gaulle. French sailors were playing soccer on the deck.

Every town had at least one,  and usually several, mosques that were always the most prominent building. This picture shows the most elaborate one. Small military installations were spaced along the waterway. They reminded me of the historic army forts in our western states having a parade ground surrounded by one-story barracks. At several locations, small ferries crossed the canal usually with a long line of waiting cars and trucks.

I started today by saying that the  canal was hard to photograph. I hope you agree that an eight-mile parade of ships in a hundred-mile ditch is a tough subject. This fellow who came on board the ship as a canal worker spent most of his day trying to sell Egyptian souvenirs and other trinkets. Maybe I should have purchased one of his pictures instead of freezing my fingers.

Mon, Mar 8   31° 27' 44"N
117 Mi. / 22355 Total Miles   031° 27' 26"E

Another early morning. Feeling the ship begin to move, I went up to the bridge at 0500 just as the captain was lamenting the fact that we had to anchor at sea last night because no pilot was available.

Our port today is about ten miles from Damietta, Egypt which has no public transportation, but there is a private guide service. At 0800 Reg, Lynne, and I sat across the table from an Egyptian entrepreneur who was an expert haggler. He wanted $75 to drive us into town, show us around, buy tea and a small sandwich, and return us to the ship in three hours. Although I don't like haggling, I think we did well. The final deal was, drive us into town and pick us up at 1600 for $30. Agreed?

Agreed. So off we went on a wild taxi ride straight out of the movies. Damietta has no traffic signals; they aren't needed because the car with the loudest horn has the right-of-way. Speed bumps are their specialty. Even the main roads have them at each intersection.

Before leaving us our guide insisted that he show us Damietta's claim to fame. He took us to the spot where the Nile River, the world's longest, empties into the Mediterranean. Actually, because the Nile fans out, there are several places where this happens, but it was still a worthy sight. It's too bad the boat picture is not in color. More than fifty boats lined the harbor and were painted in bright vivid colors like this one. Saleed said that each town uses a different motif for their fleet. Each morning men wait along the shore hoping to be hired for a days work on these fishing boats.

Saleed left at 1100 and Reg and Lynne took off on their customary long walk of discovery. At every port they seem to follow the same pattern. Fortified with bread and cheese from the ship, they set out to find the unusual, shunning the familiar tourist attractions. They would feel imprisoned on the land tours from a regular cruise ship. I set out to discover Damietta.

We had been dropped off in a section of town which fronts on the Mediterranean. In summer it will be jammed with vacationers and tourists but today only a few couples wandered the beach. Down the street was a small marketplace where live chickens shared space with

half a cow waiting to be carved up for dinner. One or two dark cafes provided a refuge for Arab men, some dressed in shirt and pants, some in flowing robes, to sip their sweet tea. No women allowed here. On the corner an open air bakery with charcoal oven going full blast produced fresh pita bread and delicious smells.

The residential area was deserted. Block after block of vacant three story buildings were shuttered. Saleed had said they would be overflowing with visitors from Cairo in three months. An apartment can be rented for four months for $1000, and with both the Nile and the Mediterranean within walking distance it sounded idyllic, but it isn't. Only the main street is paved, the side streets were simply a dirt or sand ally. Litter and trash were everywhere and a close inspection showed buildings, sidewalks, and most of the infrastructure to be in poor condition.

Again, the mosque stood out in stark contrast. It was centered on the main avenue surrounded by grass and palm trees. At noontime the call to prayer could be heard throughout the city but strangely, no one paid any attention. I don't know what I expected, but nothing happened.

Damitta is not a tourist town and I probably drew some attention as a westerner, but the few people that were on the streets seemed friendly with even an occasional smile. Only once did a small girl and her older sister approach me with their hands outstretched for money. I did not respond.

At 1530 we met Saleed back at the agreed spot and he called for a car to return us to the ship. We waited and waited and continued to wait. Small talk turned to worried talk and without the warm sun, a chill set in. When Saleed's cell phone battery went dead, Reg, Lynne, and I decided to look for a taxi if nothing appeared by 1700. Shore leave expired at 1900 and freighters don't wait. Like a Grade B movie plot, at 1655 our car came flying out of the dust, horn blasting and driver apologizing for being late, but swearing to get us back to the ship in time. On the return trip I wasn't sure whether we were destined for the ship or the morgue, but we made it.

So ends our trip through the Arab countries. This book is not the place for a discussion of religion and I am not foolish enough to conduct one. I will only observe that it tends to separate us by suspicion and distrust, which I doubt was the intent of its Creator(s).

Tomorrow we begin a new chapter and a new phase of history dominated by exploration. Welcome to the Mediterranean.

CHAPTER TEN

Mediterranean Sea
⇒ Malta ⇒ La Spezia ⇒

Tue, Mar 9   32° 52′ 48″N
294 Mi. / 22649 Total Miles   027° 00′ 42″E

Not only our chapter and sea have changed, but our climate has brought us back to the realities of winter. When the ships heating system was turned on today, a strange smell swept through the air ducts. The captain said something about a burned-out bearing and now all the outside doors are open for ventilation. This might be a cold night.

We are now well into the Mediterranean Sea. North of us are the countries of Turkey and Greece and to our south, on the African continent is Libya. Most of the early seafarers got their keels wet here in the Mediterranean. Let's look at their accomplishments.

Early Explorers
Life on this ship is usually both comfortable and predictable. In contrast, let's look at some early explorers to see who they were and what challenges they faced. Our record of explorers could stretch from prehistoric man stepping out of his cave to Neil Armstrong stepping onto the moon, but we have pared the list down to just a few of the early seafarers.

1000 Lief Ericsson, a Viking from Norway is thought to be the first European to set foot on the American continent. He left Greenland where his father, Eric the Red, had established a settlement, around 1000 AD and sailed west reaching Labrador. In Labrador natives killed his brother. He left no permanent settlements.

1492 Christopher Columbus sailed west trying to find a shorter route to the Indies. Instead he reached what we now call the Caribbean Sea. Between 1492 and 1505 he made four voyages and established several settlements.

1497 Amerigo Vespucci, the man for whom our country is named had a questionable career. He claimed to have led four voyages to the New World and on one of them to have explored the American mainland. Although he did serve as a navigator on one excursion, there is little evidence to support his other claims. Evidently he was a better writer than explorer. In 1503 he published a vivid and convincing description of his travels which persuaded the map makers of his time to give America Amerigo's name.

1519 Ferdinand Magellan did not make it all the way, but he commanded the first round-the-world expedition.   He was an experienced Portuguese captain who received the support of Spain for his venture. On September 10, 1519, with 240 men and five ships, he set sail to find a shorter route to Asia. Almost at once conflicts arose between the Portuguese captain and his Spanish crew resulting in delay, mutiny and death. In October 1520 with three remaining ships he passed through what is now called the Straight of Magellan at the southern tip of South America. From there he sailed across the Pacific for eighty-nine days without fresh food or water resulting in more loss of life. The expedition reached Guam in March and Magellan died in April during a battle with the natives.   Three years after their departure, only one ship and seventeen survivors from the original expedition limped back to Spain.

1524 Giovanni da Verrazzano was an Italian sailing under the Flag of France who was also looking for a northwest passage. He explored much of the east coast of America ranging from the Carolinas to Newfoundland. He is thought to be the first European to enter New York Bay which is why we passed under the Verrazano Narrows Bridge when we left the city.

1607 Henry Hudson thought that a route to China lay to the north and during a span of four years he made four voyages searching the northeast coast of North America. He may not have found the fabled Northwest Passage but he found the Hudson River, Hudson Strait, and Hudson Bay.

1769 James Cook, a British Naval captain, considered one of the greatest explorers, made three voyages to the Pacific. With a background in surveying, he added much to our geographical knowledge of that vast unknown area. He discovered Australia, New Zealand, and many smaller pacific islands including Hawaii. He even changed exploration itself by seeking peaceful relations with the natives and caring for the welfare of his crews. Nevertheless, like most others, he died a violent death when he interceded in a dispute between his crew and some Hawaiians.

We have explored only a small corner of the world of explorers. They and their men risked their lives for fame, fortune, trade, religion, and sometimes, even exploration. We are their beneficiaries.

Wed, Mar 10   35° 05' 28"N
557 Mi. / 23206 Total Miles   017° 39' 27"E

Usually I find only the chief mate on duty when I visit the bridge before breakfast. Today the captain, chief mate, chief engineer, and electrician were there. I thought it concerned the heating problem that we had yesterday which now seems to be fixed. No, the captain took me over to the computerized charts and pointed to the screen. "This is why we gather." I looked at the screen and followed his finger about five hundred miles up the Adriatic Sea and there to the right of Italy lay the country of Croatia, home to all these officers, and this is as close as they get.

I then received a glowing description of Croatia seemingly written by a tourist agent. Did you know that the Dalmatian dog originated in Dalmatia, now called Croatia? Did you know that Croatia was the first country to recognize America after our revolution? That some stone for the U.S. Capitol and CIA Buildings came from Croatia, and that they have some very exclusive resorts recently visited by Bill Gates? That's what they told me.

Here is more breaking news.  Criss just came in to clean the room and told me that the wife of the chief engineer will be on board for the next week. Yet our quota of lovely women will remain at two. Sadly, Lia is leaving to stay in Malta as planned.

I believe I said earlier that Singapore was not my kind of town, too materialistic. Let me present a town suitable to my tastes –Malta. However, let's be specific. Malta is a country consisting of a small group of islands about one hundred miles south of Sicily. Because of its central location in the Mediterranean, seemingly every civilization throughout the ages has occupied it including Greek, Roman, Arab, and Great Britain. It even served as a U.S. military base during the Second World War.

Valletta is the capitol but because of our late arrival we could only visit the port city of Marsaxlokk, difficult to pronounce but lovely

to look at. This picture was washed out by the setting sun, but it attempts to show an inviting beach, ringed by palm trees and a main street filled with small shops and restaurants. Out of view is a promenade that invites one to walk for several miles along aptly named Pretty Bay.

Last year Lynne and Reg had spent a month on Malta so opted to eat dinner on the ship. I wanted to get some daylight pictures, so as soon as passports were available, off I went. This bay was just ten minutes from the ship. The warm setting sun, the signs in English, the friendly faces, all said, this is my town.

Young boys were warming up for this evening's soccer game. Young girls were coyly watching. One-way narrow streets lined with medieval fronts invited exploring. We are worlds away from Singapore.

Being a sovereign nation, Malta has her own currency and postage stamps. I had a half dozen post cards to be mailed. An obliging shop keeper readily accepted my U.S. dollars for both stamps and a phone card to call Marise. He had no U.S. change offering candy instead, but I preferred the Maltese coins he gave me and will add them to my bag of world coins. Sorting them out will make a good rainy day project for my grandchildren.

Wanting to make use of the sun I delayed calling Marise and set out on a wandering trip through Marsaxlokk. The town is on a hillside with everything sloping toward the bay, so no chance of getting lost. As in Damietta, the tourist season had not started making it safe to walk in the street rather than cling to the narrow sidewalks. As the sun set, I reached the village church, momentarily bathed with natures twilight and man's night light.

Returning to the bay, everything had changed. The soccer game had ended. The children had disappeared. Now young lovers strolled the waterfront, watched and envied by their elders.

My only problem with Malta was lack of time. Someday it would be delightful to return and catch the old-fashioned bus to Valletta, or watch the old men play bocci, concentrating as though their life's reputation were at stake, or perhaps ramble the promenade in the sunshine, or simply sit on a bench and watch life pass by.

Thu, Mar 11   36° 01′ 42″N
190 Mi. / 23396 Total Miles   014° 29′ 04″E

My lack of time occurs in port. Captain Bozanic's lack of time occurs at sea. It seems he is always behind schedule and this morning was no exception. Shore leave expired at 0200 and we were due to leave at 0400. At 0530 nothing was happening and I decided to get up and stick my nose in the problem. I found a disgruntled captain waiting for the last container to go on, for the pilot to appear, and for the tugs to show up. Nevertheless, he offered me a cup of coffee.

Since the ship normally runs at full speed, there is no chance to make up time at sea by going faster, and officers behind schedule are grumpy officers. Criss happened to be mopping the hallway floor outside the bridge and I couldn't help but smile when I overheard the captain mutter "All we need is for the pilot to slip and break a leg."

Ultimately, all things came together and by 0800 we had left Malta and were sailing northwest off the coast of Sicily. Our next port is La Spezia, tucked up in the northwest corner of Italy, near Genoa. Like Marsaxlokk, it is a port city and our arrival is scheduled for 1500 tomorrow. Our route will take us past some interesting places which, while out of sight, are worth a mention.

Remember Pinocchio, the wooden puppet whose nose grew longer every time he told a lie? He was born on the Island of Stromboli in the mind of Italian author Carlo Collodi in 1892. We will be passing the Island of Elba, where Napoleon was exiled after his abdication in 1814. And we will be passing the one hundred-eighty foot Leaning Tower of Pisa which took two hundred years to build, and at the top tilts sixteen feet from the vertical.

La Spezia is at the same latitude as Portland, Maine. On my abbreviated walk to the bow today I noticed that the deckhands are wearing balaclavas under their helmets and heavy clothing under their brightly colored coveralls. Yellow for deckhands, red for the engine room, all with CMA CGM MANET stenciled across the back. Tomorrow we pass the French island of Corsica and at this latitude there is bound to be snow on the higher elevations. It is hard to believe that just weeks ago we were sweltering in Adelaide.

Fri, Mar 12   42° 47' 22"N
532 Mi. / 23928 Total Miles   009° 42' 15"E

Yes, there was snow on Corsica and there is more snow here in La Spezia, Italy. In U.S. western states we occasionally see snow and cactus together but in La Spezia, for the first time, I saw snow, cactus, and orange trees together. This picture was taken

from the waterfront park in La Spezia which is filled with sun-loving desert palms and cacti. Less than ten miles in the distance are the snow-covered Italian Dolomites, part of the Alps which run through southern Europe. They are a playground for skiers in winter and a cool retreat for vacationers in the summer.

You may have to take my word for it, but there are ripe oranges on these trees that line the main street of La Spezia. The secret is the Mediterranean, which moderates the climate of this seaside town enough to allow orange trees to grow all year around.

When we picked up our pilot at noon, gray skies and a raw wind greeted us, but by 1400 when I cleared the port gate, a warm sun had replaced the chill. The town center is within walking distance of the docks which is convenient, but once there, we find little of interest for the tourist. La Spezia is a working town with an excellent harbor which shelters a large Italian Navy Base.

Besides the orange trees and hedges, the main street has little to distinguish it. Yet a few blocks behind, you will find narrow alleys with sweet-smelling cafes, delectable bakeries, or best of all, shops filled with Italian chocolates. With Easter upon us, their windows were bursting with bunnies and chocolate eggs.

Walk toward the sea and you find a promenade, not as pleasant as Malta, but planted with palms and cactus. Having just talked to Marise two days ago and not having any euros for a phone card, I slowly worked my way back to the ship arriving just in time for dinner.

Reg and Lynne were still out on their exploratory walk so I was pleased to see some new faces at our table. La Spezia is the closest land port to Croatia so this is where many officers come and go.

The electrician who greeted me in New York and the 2nd engineer had left the ship and were replaced by similar titles. The first mate's wife, Larisa, had arrived and was seated at the officer's table along with Suzana, the chief engineer's wife. They were seated on either side of the captain.

Status at the officer's table is like a church pew. When someone of higher rank is added at one end, someone of lower rank lands on the floor at the other end. Denis, 3rd Engineer, and Fillip, a new Engineering Cadet were assigned to the passenger's table until the wives leave. Nationality takes precedence over rank. Higher-ranking Filipino officers eat with the Filipino crew but I attribute that to language and food preference, not discrimination.

Sat, Mar 13   43° 15′ 07″N
280 Mi. / 24208 Total Miles   008° 25′ 45″E

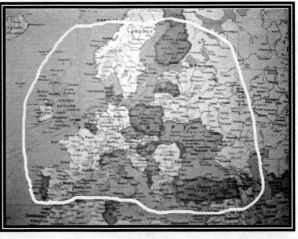

Just as we took time out to visit India, Africa, and the Middle East, let us now visit Europe. The distance from Paris to Moscow is roughly the same as from New York to Phoenix, but between Paris and Moscow we cross more than thirty countries and five thousand years of civilization. Our circle gives a rough idea of Europe's boundaries.

Europe is classified as a continent, but it is actually only a small portion of the Eurasian landmass. It covers more than four million square miles, about ten percent larger than the U.S., and it has a population of eight hundred million compared to three hundred million in the U.S.. Foolishly, I will name the five most prominent countries then run for cover: Great Britain, France, Germany, Italy, and your country.

Europe's early history is vague like elsewhere, but by 4000 BC it had a population thought to have migrated from Asia. By 2000 BC we begin to see influence from the early Greek civilization and by 200 BC, we find the Romans in power. For the next four hundred years during the birth of Christianity, the Romans ruled. They controlled the Mediterranean and developed a society dominated by a Latin culture in the West but retaining the Grecian influence in the East. By 200 AD this Greco-Roman culture was so dominant that all newborns automatically became citizens of Rome, unheard of in the small kingdoms and tribes that had previously prevailed.

However, Rome would also fall. In the third century, Germanic tribes began attacking from the north and the Huns invaded from Central Asia. By 450 AD Rome had been sacked, effectively ending the Roman Empire. But a strange thing happened. The conquerors liked what they saw in Rome so instead of changing it, they adopted it. Charlemagne, ruler of the Germanic Franks, was crowned Emperor of Rome by the Pope, thus uniting the German invaders, Rome, and the Catholic church, all under one roof called the Holy Roman Empire.

By 1000 AD Europe was in a period of transformation. Nations had not been created but communities and trade patterns were developing. The twelfth century marked the beginning of the Renaissance, a period when laws were established and the world of arts and sciences flourished.

With the establishment of country identities came provincialism and distrust. The Christian church organized the Crusades in an effort to recapture Jerusalem and other holy sites from the Muslims. Distrust and conflict between church and state occurred when regional interests conflicted with religious dogma. The onset of the catastrophic black plague which killed one quarter of the population only added to this social turmoil, but throughout the fourteenth century the Renaissance continued.

Europe was maturing and in a strange way this rivalry and restlessness led to the first voyage of Christopher Columbus in 1492. His discovery was an event that changed the world, and Europe was the leading player. No longer was the church at the focal point. Now all eyes were looking westward and a world of exploration replaced medieval Europe.

Portugal and Spain led the way gathering vast quantities of silver from the Americas which only fueled their war efforts. France emerged as the first great world power after it defeated England in the Thirty Year War, but it too collapsed during the Napoleonic Wars ending in 1815. It was not until the latter half of the 1800's that Europe found peace. Mature nations with laws had evolved, science had advanced the industrial revolution, and governments were busy laying claim to vast areas of Africa and Asia.

This period of stability did not prevail. World War I, the bloodiest war ever, and World War II turned Europe into rubble rather than Hitler's "new order." Nevertheless, Europe proved remarkably resilient. Aided by the U.S. Marshall Plan it rapidly recovered and solidified against Russia's Iron Curtain.

Today Europe is more unified than at any time in history. The European Union, ratified in 1993, eliminated most internal trade barriers and passport checks. In 1998, a new single currency called the euro was adopted and is now in use in most European countries as legal tender. Reg and Lynne believe that it is only a matter of time before England adopts the euro, effecting an even stronger bond. The future for Europe is bright.

Sun, Mar 14   37° 47' 55"N
586 Mi. / 24794 Total Miles   000° 07' 44"E

Today we continue our southerly course just off the eastern coasts of France and Spain, headed for the Strait of Gibraltar. Then its through the strait, out into the Atlantic, and a turn north, passing these countries again, only this time along their western coasts as we move north toward England.

We should note several milestones. Yesterday we began our third month at sea. Two months ago we were just leaving New York and one month ago, we were in Melbourne. And look at today's longitude; in about two hours we cross the Prime Meridian switching bearings from east to west. You remember that we lost one day on January 31st at the International Date Line. Since then we have set the clock back one hour at twelve separate time zones gaining half of it back.

This seems like a good day for touring another part of the ship. We last visited Danny's galley. Today we will work off those calories from the kitchen by walking to the bow and visiting the gym. For two months I have been trying to get a good panoramic picture of the bow. This involves climbing the forward mast high enough to get a set of three pictures panning the bow, then stitching them together on the computer. This is my best shot but it leaves much to be desired.

Imagine the bow more pointed and the horizon more rounded. Then remove the computer stitch points and you get the picture. We all agree that the bow is the best spot on the ship. It is on the lowest deck to which passengers have access. Being only about twenty feet above the ocean, on a rough day, you are at wave level.

At the aft of the ship you feel the heavy throb of the engine and hear the constant drone of generators. However, as you walk six hundred feet toward the bow, those sensations gradually evolve to serenity and the whisper of the sea. It is a strange feeling to be at the head of this giant bathtub, plowing through the water at twenty miles per hour, yet not feel the source of power. Even on a sailboat you feel the wind. Here you feel nothing, yet you move.

One of the things I shall cherish most about this trip were those warm sunny days in the southern oceans when from the bow you could gaze at the sea for eternity, trying to glimpse a flying fish or a fleeting bird. Failing a sighting, your mind would quickly wander to some pleasant dreamworld a million miles away. True peace.

However, dreaming doesn't burn calories. For that we must visit the gym and I am proud to say as the oldest person on this ship, I am one of the few who ever use the gym. The machines are always set as I left them.

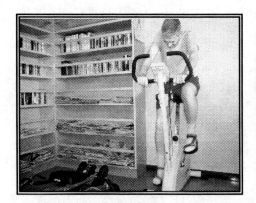 

I am equally proud of my boxing career. No losses. Rolando, a former champion boxer in the Philippines, now deckhand, saw me in the gym one day and asked if I had ever boxed. I said, "No," he said, "I teach you." I think he just wanted a dummy so he could keep in shape. Unfortunately, he left the ship in Singapore, cutting my new vocation short. No wins either.

We will pass two more milestones today. The Equatorial Circumference of the earth is 24,902.4 miles and based on our daily heading, we will pass that distance today. However we still are only in the Mediterranean because we did a little roaming around the South Pacific and other places. Our second accomplishment will be passing through the Strait of Gibraltar into the Atlantic sometime tonight. We will experience that adventure tomorrow in a new chapter.

CHAPTER ELEVEN

English Channel
⇒ Tilbury ⇒

Mon, Mar 15   37° 25′ 19″N
502 Mi. / 25296 Total Miles   009° 17′ 54″W

No, we are not in the English Channel yet, but we are headed there on a beautiful clear, windy, day. On days like this I am thankful that my desk chair does not have wheels. The ship is always rolling to a negligible degree but today we cannot ignore it. Still, the only case of sea sickness that I have heard of occurred just a few days ago when the first mate's wife came on board. Now she is obviously feeling better as she sits in his chair on the bridge.

The first mate, or chief officer is an interesting character. He is best described as an intelligent, energetic, maverick. Being a maverick is obvious with his long hair and lack of uniform, which he wears only to the dining room or when officials are on board. To be in his position at thirty-six proves his intelligence, and his energy is boundless. When off duty, he is all over the ship or listening to Croatian music in his cabin which is next to mine. He is on watch each morning and after checking the chart I usually chat with him, often about our respective countries. He is strongly pro-Croatian and while not anti-American, he says we should leave Croatia alone.

Here, he and Captain Bozanic are supervising an abandon ship drill which we had the other day. About once a week the ship's alarm goes off and the crew practices a safety drill which may involve a fire, man overboard, collision, or other emergency. We passengers are expected to go to the conference room on our level where Criss would tell us what to do in case of the real thing.   If a different alarm sounded, we would go to our lifeboat stations for an abandon ship drill.

At 2200 last night we passed through the five-mile wide Strait of Gibraltar and entered the Atlantic Ocean. Of course it was too dark for pictures of the famous Prudential Rock, but we wouldn't recognize it anyway. The view of the Prudential Logo is from the side, not from the Strait. About twenty years 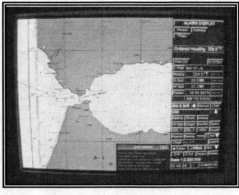 ago Marise and I crossed the Strait by ferry. As we left the shore we could see the famous side profile view, but once away from land that view disappears. The best I can do is give you a picture of the radar screen showing the Mediterranean on the right and Atlantic on the left.

Surprisingly, there were more lights on the lower African coast than the upper European coast. Because ship traffic is very heavy, it is tightly controlled and before entering we had to provide our location, destination, and any dangerous cargo listed on the ship's manifest.

The average depth of the Mediterranean is about five thousand feet, but here at its mouth it is less then one thousand feet deep. This relatively shallow mouth is no problem for shipping, but it restricts water circulation making the Mediterranean much saltier than the Atlantic which introduces our next School Day.

Salt Water

From the deck of this freighter I look in any direction and see nothing but water, yet much of the world suffers from the lack of water. Why? The question is one word and the answer is one word. Salt.

Scientists believe that as the earth cooled through geological time, water condensed from hot vapors and formed the oceans. That process is now complete; we have all the water we are ever going to get.   The hydraulic cycle exchanges water between earth and atmosphere every day, but the total amount of water on this planet is fixed and estimated at 320 billion cubic miles. Of this amount, 97% is salt water, unusable for consumption or agriculture. Of the remaining 3% which we call fresh water, 2% is frozen at the poles, leaving less than 1% of the world's water useful to man. We must protect that remaining water because that is of what we are made.

More than 65% of the human body is water, and although our sweat and tears have a high concentration of salt, our bodies cannot tolerate the intake of sea water. If I were to drink a glass of this ocean around me, my body would immediately try to dilute the salt content by draining fresh water from all my cells. Continued consumption would quickly lead to dehydration and my ultimate death.

Although the salt content of sea water varies by location and season, the average concentration is 35 parts per thousand meaning that there are 35 pounds of salt in 1000 pounds of sea water. This makes it about 220 times saltier then fresh water so the question is: if rivers of fresh water feed oceans, why are oceans salty? Remember the hydraulic cycle we mentioned earlier? When water evaporates from oceans, it leaves the salt behind. In time, that evaporated water comes back down as fresh water rain. It then runs over or through the earth picking up more salt ultimately returning to the oceans. Millions of such cycles result in a salty ocean.

It is estimated that the world's rivers carry four billion tons of salt to the oceans each year. If it were possible to extract all the salt from the world's oceans and evenly spread it over the world's land areas, it would form a layer more than five hundred feet thick.

Nature gives a clear and urgent message to mankind. Fresh water is precious. Do everything possible to keep it clean, and use it wisely.

Tue, Mar 16   45° 03' 08"N
529 Mi. / 25825 Total Miles   008° 27' 06"W

Tonight we are somewhere off the coast of France having passed Portugal and Spain earlier on our way north to England. On my way up from dinner I stepped out on deck, but found it very inhospitable with a cold damp wind and too overcast for stargazing. Such was not so only a few weeks ago when, in a tee shirt and shorts we could be very comfortable on deck after dark.

My observation begs the question, what do you do on the ship in the evening? Answer, first you spend an hour in your deck chair watching the day end as that orange globe is swallowed by the sea. Then you spend another half-hour waiting for that special moment when the clouds are postcard perfect. Now what do you do?

What are your interests? Let me list the facilities; you can determine your activity. First I shall list the facilities you will not find: bar, casino, theater, night club, bingo, or café. If you are on a freighter, these forms of entertainment probably are not your style anyway.

When the weather is good I watch the sunset as noted above. If it looks hopeful, I find a comfortable place to observe. Remember the ship is not like your home. The sun will rise and set at a different place depending on the direction of the ship. If prospects are poor, I go to my cabin and work on this book, usually for at least three hours and sometimes well after midnight if things aren't going well.

Just down the hallway is a lounge with comfortable chairs and a large table for cards, a puzzle, or any craft or hobby you may have. There is also a large TV if you are in port or near enough land for a signal. Every time I have watched, there has always been at least one English language station. If no TV, then you can watch VCR or DVD but Reg, who has checked them all out, says that most are cheap copies from Malaysia. Many mornings he has complained that just as he became deeply absorbed in the plot–poof!–it goes on the fritz.

It's unlikely, but you may be invited to the officer's lounge which is smaller, but it has a bar which I seldom see being used. With the new captain that came on in Australia, the officers now occasionally have a bottle of wine on their table at dinner.

The crew have their own recreation room with TV. When Rolando was teaching me, I went there and watched a boxing match with him. The crew usually wears sweat suits, sox and slippers when off duty, and you can always tell how busy their lounge is because they leave their slippers in the hallway.

Lynne's favorite evening pass-time is stargazing. When it was warmer, and even now all bundled up, she will sit for hours checking the heavens. The other night the mate on duty was showing her a star identification program on one of the bridge's computers, but I think she prefers to gaze and dream.

On several nights, I have gone to the bow at night. If it is a chapel in the daytime, it is an open-air cathedral at night. On one occasion the moon was full and lay low enough in the sky to create a shimmering silver walkway directly to the ship.

Another time I went because there was no moon. I found a spot that was pitch black, sheltered from the solitary bow light. Astronomers say that there are approximately six thousand stars visible from earth with the naked eye, and two thousand of those can be seen from any one place under the right conditions. Conditions were right that night. The Milky Way burst from the heavens like a billion fireworks stretched between the horizons.

Or you can go to bed.

Wed, Mar 17   50° 23' 46"N
549 Mi. / 26374 Total Miles   000° 18' 19"E

For the next few days our port stops will be coming fast and furious. Let's look at the map and schedule.

PORT	ETA BERTH	ETD BERTH
Tilbury	17/2100	18/2100
Hamburg	19/2200	20/1300
Rotterdam	21/1000	22/0100
Dunkirk	22/1200	22/2300
Le Havre	23/1130	24/0600

This schedule was posted several days ago, and in the past they have been fairly accurate. ETA is Estimated Time of Arrival and ETD is Estimated Time of Departure. The figures are date/time. On European maps Dunkirk is spelled Dunkerque.

It has been an unusual day, starting off slowly in fog and ending up with a bang of a party. I write this hoping it is coherent, if not, blame it on the party.

There was no sunrise this morning; it was lost in a fog bank on the English Channel. When I went to the bridge, Captain Bozanic said he would rather have wind and rain than fog. He spent most of the next two hours hunched over the radar scope directly in front of his chair. Around 1000 we passed between Dover on the English side and Calais in France and if you remember the song, *The White Cliffs Of Dover*, well everything was white today.

Around noon we turned left and started up the Thames River, but for the first twenty miles the mouth is so wide that even on a clear day the shores are five miles away on either side. At one point we anchored for about an hour to wait for a pilot and a higher tide. The Thames is like the Mississippi; it has a very wide mouth with many sandbars so caution is needed. By 1500 when we picked up a pilot, the fog had burned off but it was still hazy as the river channel narrowed to about three miles.

It is a six-hour journey to Tilbury Docks. Beyond that, another thirty miles up the river, is London where we hope to go tomorrow by train. Darkness came about 1700 and the river narrowed to less than a thousand feet wide. Both banks changed from rural to heavy industry with oil refineries and manufacturing. At one point I saw over a thousand new cars waiting for a delivery ship.

At 1800 it was time for dinner and this was to be a special occasion. Reg and Lynne had completed their round the world voyage!

On Christmas day they had boarded the *Manet* here at Tilbury. I first met them after boarding in New York, and back then I couldn't understand half of what they said with their proper English English. After circling the globe with them for the past two months most of their witty conversation still goes over my head, but we have had some wonderful times together.

They are truly world travelers who seem to have been everywhere. Reg is a walking encyclopedia and Lynne's charm made every meal a delight. The captain, who unfortunately was up with the pilot, had provided wine, so we drank to his health, and the health of the first mate, and the health of the second mate . . . . .   Tomorrow there should be a very healthy crew on the *Manet*. Reg and Lynne, wherever your travels take you, I wish you well, but please learn to speak proper American English.

Thu, Mar 18   51° 27' 29"N
73 Mi. / 26447 Total Miles   000° 20' 02"E

Somewhere back at the beginning of this book I mentioned that my reason for going on this trip was to find a new and stimulating experience. We have had many on this trip but today shall stand out as one of the most interesting.

Knowing that Reg and Lynne were leaving and in spite of last nights revelry, I was up at 0500 because I didn't want to miss them and a possible taxi ride into town. I was amazed to see parts of the *Manet's* decks stripped bare of containers overnight. This ship holds over two thousand containers which measure eight by eight by forty feet long.

One of the deckhands told me that
last night the stevedores unloaded
four hundred containers of wine;
now that's a lot of Cheers!

After a quick breakfast and
some final goodbyes, Reg called a
taxi and we left the ship to wait on
the wharf. After a half hour and no
taxi, I decided to walk to the gate
and try my luck at getting into London. I'm sure the taxi finally arrived
and Reg and Lynne are at home, already missing the *Manet*.

Arriving at the gate, I asked the guard for advice about going
to London for the day. He couldn't have been nicer. " Mate, just walk
down this road a bit and you'll see the train station. Take the London
train to Churchfrench Station which will put you right at the London
Bridge and if you need to change money, go to the post office across
from the train station." I could have hugged him.

By 1000 I was smack in the heart of historic London with four
hours to spend sightseeing. The Gods were with us. After calling
Marise I hopped on one of those double decker buses that tour the city
and spent the next two hours seeing Londontown.

Houses of Parliament and Big Ben

What quickly catches your attention is the time frame. The bus
guide repeatedly gave the age of buildings or monuments as eight or
nine hundred years old. My gosh, America wasn't even discovered
when these buildings and bridges were five centuries old.

Tower Bridge, not London Bridge which is in Lake Havasu, AZ

While not warm, the weather allowed good viewing from the open-air top deck of the bus. Although I didn't have time to get off, we saw most of the London highlights from afar, Trafalgar Square, Tower of London, Piccadilly Circus, and St Paul's Cathedral. We also saw some modern additions.

The world's largest ferris wheel is four hundred feet high, takes a half hour to go around, and goes so slow that it doesn't need to stop to load passengers. It has only stopped once while in operation, for a wedding at the top. And the famous London taxis, which began in the 1600's as horse-drawn coaches, are not all black anymore. Some of them sport some pretty flashy colors.

All too soon it was time to catch the train back to Tilbury. One highpoint that we missed was Buckingham Palace and the changing of the guard. Reason enough to return.

This day of new experiences continued when I arrived back at the ship. In the past, there had always been other returning passengers to share the days events with. Not any more. For the next two weeks I will not only be the oldest person on board; the Boson is next at age 52, but I will also be the only passenger and the only American on a ship with Croatians and Filipinos. A different experience indeed, and that made my day.

The passengers dining table had been set for three but the two young officers that had been eating with us on and off while the wives were on board never showed up, so I dined alone. The captain promised to continue the carafe of wine. Bon appetit!

At 1900 our tugs arrived and the pilot nudged *Manet* back into the downstream Thames current. It was too cold to stay outside for long so I sat at a chair in the lounge recording the day's events while watching the lights recede as the river widened. Soon we will be back in the English Channel turning left toward the North Sea. As the sole unpaid person on board, I couldn't help but fantasize myself as the commander in chief of this six-hundred-foot yacht and twenty-three-man crew. An experience that even Bill Gates would think twice about buying.

CHAPTER TWELVE

North Sea

⇒ Hamburg ⇒ Rotterdam ⇒ Dunkirk ⇒ Le Havre ⇒

Fri, Mar 19   53° 21′ 15″N
225 Mi. / 26672 Total Miles   004° 40′ 00″E

I'm sorry folks. We are just going to have to come back to Hamburg another day. If you think I'm going out tonight to look at the sights, forget it. This morning the weather was miserable and it has gone downhill ever since.

The North Sea is noted for its bad weather, and she showed her reputation today. The day was cold and windy making deck walking a fool's game. At lunch the captain said that it would get worse and this evening proved that the ship has a reliable weather service.

At 1400 we picked up a pilot at the mouth of the Elbe River and started the seventy-mile journey to Hamburg, Germany. For the next seven hours we slowly moved upriver passing by farmland, a few towns, and a few light industries. We also saw windmill farms; the kind that generate electricity; they were getting a windy workout today.

At 1900 I began to see the glow of lights up ahead suggesting the approach of Hamburg. Just prior to docking we passed the giant Airbus Industrie plant which manufactures airplanes and competes with Boeing. It seemed to run for miles along the riverfront.

It is now 2100 and outside the rain is coming down in buckets driven by a strong, cold wind. No night for sightseeing. However, I also note that there is no activity outside and if our departure is delayed we might see more tomorrow.

During World War II, Hamburg was a submarine base and consequently was heavily damaged by bombing raids. After the war they completely rebuilt it, so now it should be worth seeing. Cross your fingers that it rains all night keeping the stevedores home and delaying our departure, then changes to warm sunshine in the morning.

Sat, Mar 20   53° 32′ 23″N
216 Mi. / 26888 Total Miles   009° 55′ 11″E

The warm sunshine never arrived giving us a cold, but exciting day. Let's set the scene. We are in Hamburg, Germany which, if you look at your map, is north of Newfoundland and almost as far north as Juneau, Alaska. Denmark is two hundred miles north of us and Poland is about five hundred miles to the east. For the first time on this entire trip, we set our clocks ahead one hour because we had to travel east to get here.

The pilot said that Hamburg is one of the richest cities in Europe. As we sailed out of Hamburg, he pointed out a section of mansions on a hillside saying that more than one hundred billionaires live there; that's billion with a B. But I'm getting ahead of myself.

This morning the rain had stopped but it was still overcast and cold. Nevertheless, after breakfast I went to the captain's room to find out about shore leave. Loading was going well and he said I needed to be back on the ship by noon; then he called the port shuttle to take me to the gate.

Because of delays with the shuttle, I didn't leave the port until 0900 and going to Hamburg, across the river on a ferry, would be taking too much of a chance. I decided to simply go for a walk. As we have seen on several occasions, freighter travel, especially on container ships, leaves little time for sightseeing. So while I can't offer you a description of Hamburg, how about the bridge and directions to get there.

It was a good thing that we didn't go to Hamburg. Halfway through my walk it started to rain again and by the time I got back to the ship I had to change clothes. While down in the galley having a cup of coffee, the captain walked in and I told him of my adventure.

Now don't get me
wrong. I enjoyed traveling with
other passengers, but when you
are the only one on board, the
crew seems to view you more as
a guest.   Until now both
captains would not permit
passengers on the bridge when
a pilot was on board, which
makes sense.   Several

passengers roaming around the bridge at critical times could be a
problem. Now, because I am alone, the captain invited me up even
when a pilot is on board, of course I would leave if things got tight.

I took full advantage of his offer and as we returned down the
Elbe River, instead of sitting alone in the lounge, I was in a warm bridge
with panoramic windows, and privy to all the conversation and radio
messages that control this ship. For me, this was heaven.

Now you know how I got the information about the billionaires.
Here's another tidbit, the pilot addresses the captain as captain; the
captain addresses the pilot as Mr. Pilot, and there is minimal
conversation between the two. The pilot gives orders to the helmsmen
and only occasionally discusses something on the radar screen with the
captain.

Tonight we are back in a windy North Sea headed south for
Rotterdam, the world's largest shipping port.

Sun, Mar 21   53° 03' 38"N
238 Mi. / 27126 Total Miles   004° 12' 57"E

Members of the crew had said that these European ports were
the busiest time in their round the world trip. I agree; it's 2130 and I
just got back from Rotterdam. Seems like I have been out straight
since Tilbury, but it sure is interesting. Here's how the day went.

Up at six after a very windy night on the North Sea. Some rock
and roll is relaxing and conducive to sleep, last night went far beyond
that. Every time you dozed off, a series of waves would hit and vibrate
the whole ship. Everyone was complaining about lack of sleep this
morning. The morning was clear with gale force winds as we passed

several giant oil rigs out in the middle of nowhere. I wouldn't work on one of those for all the tea in China.

As we approached Rotterdam we were advised that because of rough seas, the pilot might be transferred to the *Manet* by helicopter, but by the time we got there things had quieted enough for what was still an unusual transfer. From a large pilot boat, to a small fast one, to the *Manet*.

At 1300 we entered the harbor and began a slow winding trip through a maze of waterways. We passed a set of enormous sea gates that can be closed if winds push the tides

One of two sea gates

too high. In another area we saw just one of many dry-docks available for ship repairs, which is why Rotterdam is considered one of the world's major seaports.

A half hour after docking, I started off, passport in hand but not really knowing how far I would get. It was sunny with a cold biting wind off the sea. It was Sunday, meaning businesses would close early. This was an enormous port having several gates and dozens of similar wharfs simply inviting a lone passenger to get lost after dark. On the other hand, I had nine hours of shore leave not to be wasted.

My first bit of luck occurred when the driver of a delivery truck at the *Manet* offered a lift to the gate which turned out to be almost two miles away. At the gate the attendant said there was no public transportation but he called a taxi which fortunately had a driver who spoke good English and gave me a history lesson as we drove to town.

During the war, because Rotterdam was an important seaport, the Germans flattened most of it leaving city hall which they wanted to use during their occupation of Holland. After the war Rotterdam was rebuilt. It is now going through a new rejuvenation, giving the city three distinct architectural periods.

What really pleased me was Rotterdam's friendliness toward bicycles. From the number of parked bicycles, it seems the whole country uses them. All of the main streets have dedicated bike lanes which are completely separate from the auto lanes.

What I didn't like about the city was a heavy smoking habit. One would think that bicycling and smoking do not go together, but from what I've seen, Europeans are still hooked on the habit. Would you believe, smokers and ash trays in McDonald's?

All too soon the sun slipped behind those tall buildings and people started to fade from the streets on this cold Sunday evening. I took another taxi only after making sure the driver knew the location of my gate. Moments after we arrived an old fellow with a last minute delivery of wire for the *Manet* drove up. He gave me a ride straight to the gangplank, ending a busy but satisfying day.

This is by far my latest return to the ship and it is past midnight, so goodnight. We leave at 0200 for Dunkirk, France.

Mon, Mar 22   52° 02' 07"N
83 Mi. / 27209 Total Miles   003° 10' 22"E

Yesterday, while waiting for Customs to stamp my passport, I was watching the delivery of supplies to the ship. Rotterdam, Savannah, Auckland, and Singapore are the major resupply ports so it was like Christmas morning as each department got its new supplies.

Danny's galley gets the most attention. Even before we tied up, there were two delivery trucks waiting, filled with everything from apples to yogurt, for the next three weeks. It is all lifted onto the ship by pallet, but then must be broken down and stored in the appropriate freezer. This is too much for Danny to do alone so the deckhands help, and probably help themselves a little when Danny isn't looking.

Meanwhile, the *Manet* is getting her rations for the trip across the Atlantic. Two fuel barges are tied up along side, each with an enormous hose attached to the ship's fuel tank's. Even so, it takes several hours to pump the two thousand, four hundred tons of bunker fuel needed to get to

Savannah. And that's not all she's getting. Before I left, another truck drove up and dropped off a few hundred gallons of paint in a rainbow of colors. The deckhands were not so eager to unload this cargo. It will keep them working for many months.

Today we are bound for Dunkirk, France, or Dunkerque depending on your preference. Dunkirk is famous for a military evacuation which took place during World War II. At the beginning of the war Allied troops were being driven back by the Germans and they retreated to the English Channel at Dunkirk. During a two-month period in 1940, over three hundred thousand troops were evacuated from Dunkirk to the safety of England, using every possible craft, both naval and civilian, that could cross the channel.

Today, it is a relatively minor port compared to most we have seen. This time, as we passed back through the English Channel, we were able to clearly see the white chalk cliffs of Dover that we had passed in the fog just five days ago, but they were too far off for a photo.

The weather was clear and not as windy as the past few days but strangely enough, today when it was calmer, the pilot elected to come on board by helicopter. That was fine by me and I got some good pictures from the bridge. I immediately went down to my cabin and printed a montage of them which I gave to the pilot. I think he was pleased.

I think the captain was also pleased because later he complained that the pilot had taken it with him and could he have his own copy. Of course I obliged.

It was about 1500 when we finally tied up at Dunkirk. The town is located too far from the port for a visit on this short stay, so I satisfied myself with a two-mile walk to the local Seamen's club. It didn't have all the services that some of the others had but I was able to call Marise and as usual, she has everything under control.

Tue, Mar 23   49° 28' 59"N
219 Mi. / 27428 Total Miles   000° 10' 48"E

I didn't know what to expect from Le Havre but was pleasantly surprised. It has been another busy day beginning at 0630 when I went to the bridge and found both captain and chief mate waiting for the pilot. For a change we seem to be ahead of schedule.

To enter the Le Havre port, we had to go through a lock for the first time since the Panama Canal. It certainly didn't match Panama, but it was an interesting passage and it gave me time to ask the pilot about the highlights of Le Havre. He was most helpful with his description of the city and offered me a ride into town. We had cleared French Customs in Dunkirk so I was ready when he was.

At 0930 I found myself in the middle of Le Havre looking for my bearings. Fortunately, near where the *Manet* was moored, there was a power plant with two high smokestacks that I could see from the city. The pilot had taken a number of twists and turns to get me here and I knew I could walk back, as long as I could find my way. Quite often the dock areas are quite confusing especially when there are several gates. If you are in a car, no problem, you can zip here and there. But on foot, zipping here and there takes twenty minutes to the mile.

From the sea, Le Havre didn't look very impressive, however once inside the city, I found broad tree-lined streets and several beautifully maintained parks. At one, they were mowing the grass for the first time, releasing that first fresh smell of spring. One week later and we would have been engulfed in tulip blossoms, but it was heartening just to know they were on their way. I'm not sure what to call this. A statue, a sculpture? There was no nameplate or plaque, so use your imagination; that is what art is for.

Evidently we used all our luck on the ride into town. The pilot had highly recommended the local museum, but when I got there it was closed for one day each week–Tuesday–today. C'est la vie.

I looked for a visitor center, again with no luck. Maybe this is not a tourist town; it should be.  My ramble took me down to the waterfront where hundreds of sailboats waited with their naked masts longing to be wrapped in cloth for that first fling of spring. At another waterfront, right in the center of town, there were children in a dozen sailboats learning how to play and tack at the same time.

For several hours I enjoyed meandering along the streets and canals of Le Havre, but being  unsure of the return route to the *Manet*, I decided to start home. It was a pleasant walk in the warm sun and shortly after I passed the two chimneys, the blue cranes of our ship came into view. Throughout the journey this ship, our home, has always been a welcome sight in a foreign port.

On my return I found a very quiet ship. These men have worked hard, visiting five ports in one week. I have learned that, like an airplane, the difficult part is landing and takeoff. On this ship each procedure takes hours of work and preparation, sometimes in the worst of weather. They deserve their rest.

Tomorrow we begin the final leg of this journey, but crossing the Atlantic is never a simple task, especially in March winds.

CHAPTER THIRTEEN

North Atlantic Ocean
⇒ New York

| Wed, Mar 24 | Same |
| Same | Same |

Good news and bad news, first the bad. Our 0600 departure time has been delayed. There was no significant reason, the captain only saying at lunch that loading was to blame. Our new departure time is 1500.

Now the good news. This morning I was pleasantly surprised to find slipped under my door, an e-mail from Carl and Pancha who, you remember, left the ship on February 4th at Auckland. They enjoyed New Zealand so much that they may go back for an entire season sometime in the future. I agree, it is a wonderful country and will reply to their message as soon as I return home. I haven't used the ship's e-mail because frankly, this book takes most of my time, instead, at each port I call Marise which has worked well for us.

While we wait for the ship to get underway on her Atlantic voyage, we might profitably use our time reading about all the oceans.

Oceans
If we were to view our planet from space, we would describe it as mostly blue, having white caps at either end, with some large brown islands dotting the surface. The predominant color is blue because 71% of our planet is covered with water, primarily expanses of blue that we call oceans. We have been crossing these oceans for some time now so maybe we should take a closer look at them.

Oceans of the World

Pacific Ocean	64,186,300 sq. mi.
Atlantic Ocean	33,420,000 sq. mi.
Indian Ocean	28,350,500 sq. mi.
Arctic Ocean	5,105,700 sq. mi.

Many other large bodies of water are classified as seas, gulfs, and bays, but none of them come close to the size of an ocean. We may think of the Gulf of Mexico as a large body of water. In actuality it is only one tenth the size of the smallest ocean, the Arctic. Map makers often split the Pacific and Atlantic Oceans at the equator calling them North Pacific, South Pacific, North Atlantic, and South Atlantic, but any way you cut it, the Pacific Ocean is by far the largest body of water on our planet.

The Pacific Ocean is also the deepest body of water. The Mariana Trench, near Guam in the western Pacific, has a depth of 35,840 feet. If we placed Mount Everest on the bottom of this trench, its summit would still be more then a mile below the surface. With its massive size and depth, the Pacific Ocean holds more than half the world's water.

Size is only one aspect in the importance of oceans. London, England is four hundred miles closer to the North Pole then Montreal, Canada. Yet its average January temperature is warmer by 22.5 degrees. Why? Every day, billions of gallons of Atlantic Ocean water are carried north by the Gulf Stream from the tropics toward the arctic, warming England and Ireland as they pass. "And what force powers the Gulf Stream?" you might ask. It is the Coriolis Force which drives ocean currents clockwise in the Northern Hemisphere and counterclockwise in the Southern Hemisphere. Here is my feeble attempt to explain the Coriolis Force.

Picture yourself standing on the equator facing east. Even though you are standing still, because of the earth's rotation, you and the patch of ground you are standing on, are actually traveling at over one thousand miles per hour. Remember, the circumference of the earth is 25,000 miles and you will rotate that distance every 24 hours. This force of rotation tends to move the ocean currents in a whirlpool fashion and is also responsible for the spiral movement of hurricanes.

One final bit of trivia having nothing to do with oceans. Just as we race forward at 1,000 miles per hour at the equator, (and only at the equator because our rotational speed decreases as we move toward the poles where it is zero), we and our planet are also racing through space at 66,000 miles per hour as we circle the sun every year. Tired?

Promptly at 1500, *Manet* cast off her ties to Europe and eased out into the English Channel, her bow pointed toward America. Just another country for her, home for us.

Thu, Mar 25   49° 04' 22"N
312 Mi. / 27740 Total Miles   006° 43' 38"W

Our faithful ship plowed westward all night, but at 0530 I awoke to the silence of drifting without power. Curiosity soon got the best of me and I went to the bridge to find the captain and first mate drinking coffee. "We were wondering how long it would take you to get up here? Are you in a hurry to get to New York?" was my greeting.

Next time you have car problems, it might ease your pain knowing that even a massive ship like this can have a mechanical breakdown. And out here you don't simply call a tow truck. Instead, we have six excellent mechanics on board who were roused out of bed to discover a broken cylinder bolt. That was the reason for our silence.

As I suspected, they have the tools, parts, and the knowledge to fix all things and by the time breakfast was over, *Manet's* muscle had been repaired and we were underway again. I would speculate that if required, they could even fix a broken marriage.

If we equate the engine room to the muscle, then we must surely liken the bridge to the brain and today would be a good time to take our final tour of the Manet; let's go right to the top, the bridge. On a passenger ship, if lucky, you may be given a guided tour of the bridge when nothing is happening. During the past-busy week in Europe, it seems I have spent half my waking hours on the bridge.

This is the command center of the captain, the man on the left if you weren't sure. He has a very short commute, one flight of stairs. From this penthouse, with its panoramic windows, we have literally seen the world. There is an administrative office on the deck below us where much of the paperwork is done, but it is here that the mental work is done.

While in port, the bridge is locked, but about an hour before sailing, a key is turned and this control center comes alive. Electronic equipment is turned on and checked as are communication channels soon to be needed for relaying information. The pertinent charts are laid out and appropriate computer information is updated. Finally the most vital appliance of all is activated, the coffee pot.

 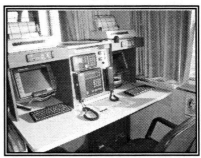

By the time the pilot arrives all is ready. Working together, the captain instructs the bosun in his job of casting off the lines while the pilot coordinates the two tugs, one fore, and one aft. In slow motion we begin to move. Pulled by the tugs, *Manet* inches away from the pier as her lines are winched in and stored for the next port.

Now the pilot settles in to guide the ship through harbor waters that only he is familiar with. Ship traffic is heavy and always changing, as are sandbars and other port obstacles. While he gives compass direction to the helmsmen, he also gives towing direction to the tugs, and slowly we work our way out to open waters. Sometimes it is only a few miles; in Hamburg it was seventy miles, but ultimately we arrive at a point where the captain takes over and the pilot returns to port via the pilot boat.

Now the throttle is put at sea speed and new ocean charts are brought out. Now one inch equals one hundred miles instead of one mile, as on the port charts. It may be for a day or ten days, but a routine settles in on the bridge as we move toward our next destination at twenty-four miles per hour.

Our location coordinates are penciled in on the chart every four hours when the officer's change watch. This is the first thing I look at on my bridge visits and as the marks get closer to our destination, activity on the bridge picks up again.

Flags for the new country are brought out and placed in ready to be unfurled before the pilot comes aboard. When he arrives by pilot boat, the whole procedure begins again, in reverse. Hours later we are tied to a new pier, in a new port, in a new country. The engine is quiet, the stevedores are on board doing their work, and the doors to the bridge are locked.

 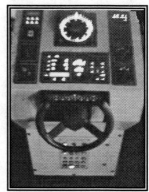

I hesitate to leave the bridge without describing it at night when it appears entirely different. In the daytime, our eyes scan the horizon to look for ships and other sights of interest. At night we still look out the dark windows for lights from other ships or shores, but not for navigation. Now we concentrate on the radar screen plus a myriad of other gauges and dials, all glowing red for night vision.

Try as we might, the first mate, who is an excellent photographer, and I have tried to get a good picture of these gages at night. If we use flash, the red is washed out, if we don't use flash, the red is blurred without a tripod. Our best effort is shown in the above right photo, when he turned the light intensity as high as possible.

The chart room at the rear of the bridge has normal lighting which is dimmed at night, but in addition, a curtain is drawn across to keep that white light out of the working bridge area. All this gives the effect of entering a dark movie theater when you visit the bridge at night. At first you see nothing, but as your eyes adjust, you are surrounded by glowing red light from all directions, similar to an airline cockpit, but much larger.

Hours spent on the bridge will fill a large chapter in my book of memories. This privilege alone is enough to make me a confirmed freighter traveler.

Fri, Mar 26   46° 11' 40"N
586 Mi. / 28326 Total Miles   018° 35' 17"W

According to today's posting, we are scheduled to pick up the New York pilot at 0400 and be tied up by 0600 on April 1st. We are nearing the end of our journey but new things continue to happen. Last night at dinner, a dish slid off the table for the first time. Exciting! This wild North Atlantic is upholding her reputation.

It was too cold and windy to stay out for long, but from the warmth of the bridge, I watched as a dozen large birds swooped and glided all day, just off our starboard side. A strong wind was driving down from the north, hitting the wall of containers on the *Manet* then being forced upwards. It was in this updraft, just one-hundred feet from the window, that displaying matchless grace with little effort, they frolicked and soared for hours, like children at play.

Changing topics, I would like to bring up a subject that has bothered me for some time and should concern all of us, the plight of today's seamen. For all of history, seafarers have transported our goods around the world leaving their families for months, even years at a time. All they ask is fair pay, reasonable working conditions, and a chance to leave the ship at port for relaxation, and a call to their family at home. Fair enough, you say; this is their chosen profession.

The situation that exists today is not what they signed on for. Since September 11, port after port has closed its gates to seamen wanting to leave the ship for a few hours or to return home after their contract has been filled. We have on board this ship two Filipino crew members who have completed their nine month contracts and were scheduled to leave the ship in New York and fly home for their earned vacation. They have been told that they will not be permitted to leave the ship until reaching Australia, six weeks from now.

These men are no more of a terrorist then I am, yet they are being treated like prisoners. The Seamen's Church Institute of New York found that over a typical one week period on the east coast, roughly one thousand seamen are denied shore leave.

The President of the North American Maritime Ministry Association recently testified at a U.S. Homeland Security hearing regarding new regulations for vessels and terminals. "Life on board is difficult enough because of the long periods of isolation. But to be denied the ability to call home, do some shopping for personal needs, or relax away from the ship is really inhumane treatment."

On July 1, 2004, the new International Ship and Port Security Code will go into effect. It requires the development of plans to counter security threats on ships and in ports. It will apply to some fifty-thousand ships and twenty-thousand worldwide ports. No doubt it will mean tighter restrictions and further confinement of seamen. It may even limit the access of port chaplains who provide support and ministry to visiting ships.

There is another problem which certainly does not apply to the *Manet*. Elsewhere in this shipping business, usually around the edges, hundreds of seafarers are actually abandoned each year. Unscrupulous operators purchase a ship, hire a crew, make a few trips and if not profitable, disappear, leaving the crew without pay, support, or the funds to return home.

Fortunately, there is an organization, the International Christian Maritime Association (www.icma.as), which is able to provide limited help. This is a group of Christian Centers and other Seamen's Welfare Agencies that has branches at most major ports. They were the ones that provided us with a ride back to the ship on several occasions, but their ministry and relief work is far more important. Often, they are the only familiar and friendly sight that greets a seafarer when he enters a strange port. They provide a vital service to a forgotten group. I hereby make a pitch for their support.

We live in an age of terrorism which we must guard against, but America was built by men like this. They are simply looking for a place to rest, and in full view of the Statue of Liberty, we shut the door.

Sat, Mar 27   43° 22' 37" N
567 Mi. / 28893 Total Miles   029° 27' 41"W

Freighter travel is not superior to cruise ship travel. After reviewing some of my writing, it appears I may have inferred that. If so, I apologize. They each cater to a certain clientele, and it is obvious from the numbers that cruise ships are far more popular than freighters.

While browsing the Internet prior to my trip, I came across this quiz to determine one's suitability for freighter travel. It was commissioned for the travel industry several years ago and seemed to fit my needs. See how you score with a yes or no answer; find out if freighter travel is right for you.

1. Do you have many friends?

2. Must you keep abreast of current events?

3. Are you wealthy?

4. Do you crave gourmet meals?

5. Do technical subjects tend to bore you?

6. Do you enjoy social gatherings?

7. Do you prefer guided tours?

8. Do you like to be waited on?

9. Do you have any serious health problems?

10. Are you uncomfortable when alone?

If you answered eight or more questions with a "no" you are a good candidate for freighter travel. If you said no to all of them, you are invited to join the prestigious organization that prepared this study, the Massachusetts Institute of Scientific Facts Involving Travel Scenarios.

Wanting to find out if my psychological profile was right for freighter travel, I took the quiz, answered all questions with a no, and now look forward to their monthly magazine entitled *MISFITS*.

Sun, Mar 28   40° 32′ 01″N
598 Mi. / 29491 Total Miles   040° 27′ 58″W

Please don't pester my publisher with parcels of petty papers pleading for packets of popular pertinent periodicals printed by MISFITS. It was a joke, but my questions are apropos.

Technically speaking, today we are smack dab in the middle of the Atlantic and it is as calm as a millpond. Our captain is both surprised and pleased. For a change, the ship is ahead of schedule; the crew is not under pressure, and the sun is out. What more could a master want?

During this trip, I used a small digital recorder and a notebook to remember events and thoughts for later use. Most entries were deleted or crossed out as I used them, but there are still a few that don't fit anywhere. Today's title: Potpourri Page.

Item: If you are taking a trip of any length, buy a map and hang it on the wall. I also had a GPS unit and used it to mark our daily position, then connected the dots. Looking at the overall route was helpful and prompted many discussions with crew and fellow passengers. The GPS unit was nice but not necessary. That information is always available on the bridge.

Item: Bring a small roll of double-sided tape for hanging your map and a million other uses.

Item: At this time you don't need a visa for Egypt. At Damietta, they gave us a temporary port pass. However, you do need a visa for Australia. This can change, check with your agent.

Item: The only shot I needed was for yellow fever but that, of course, depends on your itinerary.

Item: Learn a little Filipino

Word	Phonetic	Meaning
Magandang Umaga	MA GAN DA OU MA GA	Good Morning
Magandang Tanghali	MA GAN DA TA HALLI	Good Afternoon
Magandang Gabi	MA GAN DA GABI	Good Night
Kumosta Ka	KUM O STA KA	How are you?
Salamat	SAL A MAUT	Thank You

Thank goodness the Croatian officers could speak English; that's a tough language.

Item: Having information about future ports is always helpful. We had none, so I bought a cheap notebook and with the help of my fellow passengers, gathered maps and other useful information at local tourist centers. The books were left in the lounge and should be of value to future passengers.

Item: Favor darker clothing. The ship is constantly washed by salt air and occasionally dusted by diesel ash.

Item: If you use one, bring your own face cloth.

Item: I had little success with a short wave radio and frankly, after a month at sea I lost interest in "worldly" affairs.

Item: I was fortunate, having no health problems, not even a twinge of seasickness. If necessary, the port agent can be helpful in arranging an emergency doctor or dental visit. Talk to the captain.

Item: Circumnavigating the globe can be done in two directions. One minor consideration is time changes. We set our clock back twenty-four times meaning that on twenty-four nights we had an extra hour of sleep. We lost a day at the International Date Line, but who cares about a day, it's that extra hour of sleep that feels good. In the eastbound direction you do just the opposite, gain an extra day and lose twenty-four separate hours.

Item: If possible, have the ship's stamp put in your passport. At some ports they gave us a port pass. Where they didn't, it was helpful when returning from town to have proof that I was a passenger on the *Manet* stamped right in my official passport.

Item: As of this date the world's largest ship is the *Jahre Viking*, a 1,503 foot long, 226 foot wide, 565,000 ton oil tanker. The 90,000 ton aircraft carrier *Abraham Lincoln*, is 1,092 feet long and the *Manet* is 642 feet long.

Item: When I was writing, I left my cabin door open. Many of the tidbits of information in this book came through that open door.

Item: When dining, service to the officers takes priority over service to the passengers.

Item: When returning from shore leave, bring back a candy bar for the crew member who will greet you at the gangplank.

Item: If you are at all proficient with a digital camera, bring it. Better still, also bring a small printer. Photos of activities on board are much appreciated.

Item: With your camera, take and print a small picture of your ship and keep it with you on shore leave. It might be of help in an emergency, or with a taxi driver who can't understand you.

Item: The *Manet* has a carrying capacity of 2,272 containers. There are firm orders for ships that will carry 8,400 containers and South Korea is preparing its ports for vessels capable of carrying 12,000 containers.

Item: On several occasions I used my pocket voice recorder and digital camera to record or photograph directions while walking into town. This made it easier to get back to the ship. Sort of like dropping bread crumbs. Once safely back on board, everything is erased. This method can be used in every day life anytime you are in unfamiliar surroundings.

The remainder of this page is left blank for your ideas or any others I might think of before this book goes to press.

Mon, Mar 29   41° 47′ 01″N
567 Mi. / 30058 Total Miles   051° 13′ 20″W

Today is what winter in the Atlantic should be. We were headed due west on a course for New York on a placid sea. Last night that all changed, as did our course, to avoid a storm. We have detoured about a hundred miles to the north, toward Labrador, to avoid a strong low pressure storm to our south. Even so, we are rocking today and once again the temperature is bitter cold.

Every morning before breakfast, I stop in at the galley to say good morning to Danny and his assistant, Oscar. Today Danny had a gift for me; a framed photo of the *Manet* which he had purchased somewhere along the way. To say the least, I was extremely moved. My voice quivered as I finished reading the note taped on the back.

HONORABLE MR. ROBIN HARTLEY
American Engineer
Mr. Bob
As I promise... A souvenir...
A place where we had met.
Thank You
GOD BLESS AMERICA
MABUHAY PHILIPPINES
(Signed)
DANILO A. OCHOA
Cook – CMA CGM MANET

Friendships will be one of the fondest rewards of this trip. Although we will never meet again, it is comforting to know that somewhere in this world there is a man who was pleased, as I was, that we met.

I hope you enjoyed School Days and learned a thing or two about our world. These essays were meant to be brief introductions to a subject, each one quickly skimming over a lot of material, but as the man said, "You ain't seen nuthin yet." Our last topic ties it all together. It may be presumptuous of me but here is our genesis on one page.

History in a Nutshell

If all the volumes written about history were loaded aboard this ship, no doubt we would sink straight to the bottom. To lighten our load, I have taken the liberty of condensing all of Time into one page. We are going to be flying down through the ages very fast, so I suggest that you turn up the light, turn off the TV, and concentrate on this next article.

The Big Bang created our universe. Physicists say that between ten and fifteen billion years ago a massive explosion created all the matter that exists in our universe today. During the next ten billion years the ensuing gas and dust swirled around until the force of gravity began to pull specs of it together. About five billion years ago our solar system, the sun and its nine planets, was formed by these gravitational forces. The earth bubbled and boiled for eons until the first one-cell form of life appeared in this soup more than three billion years ago. These life forms moved from the oceans to dry land half a billion years ago and slowly evolved into plants, animals, and birds. The first human species descended from African apes five million years ago and we think that sixty thousand years ago humans were advanced enough to sail to, and colonize Australia. China claims the first modern civilization beginning about six thousand years ago and you know the rest. The birth of Christianity and other religions, the renaissance, the discovery of the new world, the industrial revolution, and so on, brings us to today, all in one paragraph.

THIS EVENT HAPPENED	YEARS AGO
Big Bang creates universe	15,000,000,000
Earth and our solar system created	5,000,000,000
One-cell life appears in oceans	4,000,000,000
Multi-cell life moves to land	500,000,000
First human species	5,000,000
Humans colonize Australia	50,000
China has earliest modern civilization	5,000
Columbus discovers New World	500
Atomic bomb developed that can destroy humanity	50
World Trade Center attack changes our way of life	5

Obviously the above table is very rough so here is your key to using this knowledge. If you are taking your college entrance exams and are good at padding ideas, I suggest you memorize the descriptive paragraph, fatten it up with lots of cliches, and you just might squeak by. On the other hand, if you are at a cocktail party and your audience has had a few drinks, you can quote tidbits from the table and sound positively brilliant.

Tue, Mar 30   41° 06′ 03″N
594Mi. / 30652 Total Miles   062° 39′ 51″W

Tomorrow we arrive in New York. Today is a day for summation. On April 1st we will have been at sea eighty-one days having spent considerable time, energy, and fortune on this venture. What have we accomplished beyond filling our passport full of stamps?

From a negative viewpoint we have accomplished nothing. The *Manet* would have made this trip with or without us, and although we were on board, we contributed nothing to the mission. However, you should know by now that I don't subscribe to the negative view.

Considering nothing else, we have gone around the world. Transportation has come a long way since Magellan's first circumnavigation; today the world is traveled every day by ship and plane. On the other hand, of the six billion people on this earth, how many have gone completely around it in one trip? You have. And I guess this is as good a place as any to talk about participation.

Throughout this book I often shift between the personal pronouns "I, my" and "we, our." My preference would have been to use the plural "we, our" all of the time. I always needed your participation to carry out the storyline, but there were times when the plural was grammatically awkward. If reading will take us anywhere our mind will accept, having reached the final pages in this book metaphorically qualifies you as a global traveler.

But was it worth it? Of course my answer is yes, but I must go on to justify that reply. When we were young, they told us to get a good education because "they can never take it away from you." The same reasoning applies to travel inasmuch as travel is not only educational, but an experience. School Days and this trip have given us the tangible rewards of knowledge and participation. The adventure has also given us an intangible world of memories.

Forevermore, you will remember, as I do, the many ports we have visited and all the new experiences we have had during the past weeks. It seems so long ago that we watched in biting cold, as the Verrazano Narrows Bridge slipped away in darkness. Since then we have been through blistering heat in Adelaide, pelting rain in Auckland, and sweltering humidity in Noumea.

We will remember what it is like to live in a cabin high above the sea, have a delicious cup of coffee with three butter cookies in the morning, and be lulled to sleep at night by the throb of the engine. We will long for the serenity of those warm afternoons as we gazed from the bow at the Southern Ocean, searching for flying fish or, failing that, the meaning of life.

Strange ports have opened our eyes to different cultures, natural oddities, and manmade wonders. Stimulating discussions at the dinner table have broadened our knowledge and sharpened our thoughts. Lighter conversations with crew and local townspeople have reinforced our belief that most people are good, simply wanting to live their lives in peace. And life at sea is no longer a mystery.

Somewhere near the beginning of this book I said, "From past travels I know that an extended trip in unfamiliar surroundings strips away our blanket of routine, producing a stimulating experience. That is my objective." It has been a stimulating experience, I have fulfilled my objective.

For the past eighty days I have not driven a car, answered a telephone, or read a newspaper. Not many days from now I will miss those freedoms. I will miss watching the sunrise with the first mate and my daily banter with Criss. I will miss my afternoon walk to the bow, standing on the monkey deck, seeing nothing and everything at the same time. I will miss the excitement of discovering a new town, and the relief of returning to the ship.

I will miss all these things, but in the future I will experience them over and over as my mind drifts back to *Manet* and the sea. Descending the gangplank tomorrow and returning to Times Square will close the circle and complete the journey, but within that circle there is a world of memories, and like education, " they can never take it away from you."

CHAPTER FOURTEEN

Home Port
⇓

Wed, Mar 31   40° 28' 59"N
514 Mi. / 31166 Total Miles   073° 46' 05"W

AMERICA! We can hear it, smell it, and almost feel it, but from here we can't see it. We are anchored outside New York harbor, just north of Ambrose light ship, but fog limits our visibility to half a mile. It is ironic that after a hectic trip around the world we spend the final day drifting at anchor.

Being ahead of schedule, we traveled all night at the reduced speed of seventy-five RPM, about twenty miles per hour. Incidently, seventy-five RPM equals seventy-five thumps per minute from the engine which equals the normal heart beat which may account for why we sleep so well at sea. That's just my theory, don't bet the farm on it.

At 0530 I went to the bridge where both captain and first mate had their eyes glued to their radar screens. At that time we were passing the eastern end of Long Island. I was back on the bridge at 1030 as we set our anchor and called the pilot station to confirm our arrival. There was no mistaking the American voice at the other end, strong, with a little bit of swagger and a lack of formality. We are home.

After lunch I took my final walk to the bow. Every daily activity that had become routine was savored today as something special, knowing it was for the last time. Seeing *Manet* chained to an anchor on a cold gray afternoon seemed an injustice to this lady that had carried us through dancing waves on sunlit afternoons.

Then there were the closing rituals. Alfredo gave me a declaration form to fill out for Customs and presented me with a bill for sixteen dollars for a case of beer. Criss helped me take down "our" map which now had a solid green line running across it. I retrieved my forgotten suitcase and stuffed it with  none of the care that Marise and I had given it three months ago. I was going home and growing restless with our delay.

Of course the best way to combat restlessness is to have a party and Captain Bozanic was gracious enough to provide just that, and in my honor. Wow! As I entered the mess hall Danny, Oscar, and Criss were bringing out the salads, meats, vegetables, and a fresh baked turkey, all topped off by a cake that said "Thank you Mr. Bob." Thank you for what? I should be the one to say thank you to these men who gave me a lifetime of memories.

At my table sat Philip and Steven, two engineering cadets, who had been sharing the table of a lone passenger. I had come to know them well but always felt guilty drinking wine while they sipped water. For the first time, the captain allowed them to share my bottle. Tonight, a good time was had by all.

Equating these men to family is overstating it, but I have learned to respect their ability and certainly enjoyed their company for the past twelve weeks.

After dinner I went to the crew's recreational room where they were watching New York television. This is the other half of the family, different, but equally honored and respected. These are the men that care for *Manet* as a mother cares for her child. Without them, *Manet* would be lifeless. I thank them all.

The celebration is over, the bags are packed, time to rest for an early morning departure.

Thu, Apr 1   40°41′ 14″N
18 Mi. / 31184 Total Miles   074° 00′ 34″W

On January 12th we left in bitter cold. On April 1st we returned in dense fog. I was hoping for a clear morning so we could get a good picture of the Verrazano Narrows Bridge, but that was not to be. The roadway lights were barely visible and the tower tops were lost in fog.

I will have to rely on my memory of a clear summer day forty-two years ago when, as a Junior Engineer working on the bridge, I had a chance to visit the top of the six hundred-ninety-foot Staten Island tower. On that day I could see forever, this morning we could barely see the ship's forward crane. By the way, did  you know that in summer, because of cable expansion, the bridge deck is twelve feet lower than in winter.

North of the bridge we were joined by a second pilot and two tugs. In conditions like this the pilot earns his money. By 0630 he had us securely tied to the same pier that we had left eighty-one days ago.

My trip to the galley for breakfast resembled a receiving line as I, all too awkwardly, parted with these former strangers, now friends. Customs was the final hurdle. They simply asked if it was a good trip, stamped my passport, and I was free to go.

At 0830 after a final goodbye to Captain Bozanic and the first mate, Criss helped carry my bags off the ship and I found myself outside the port gate walking toward the subway. One hour later, having purchased my train ticket and called Marise, I relaxed in Penn Station. Symbolically, to close the circle, I should have walked the eight blocks to Times Square, the "Official Ending Point" of our journey, but at the time, a cup of hot coffee seemed more significant.

Twenty-two hours later the cold grey fog of Manhattan had given way to warm Florida sunshine. Now for sure the journey was over when my bride of forty-eight years met me at the Kissimmee train station. Our sixty-mile drive back to the RV shrank to sweet moments as each of us spilled out our experiences of the past three months. To many of her questions I replied "read the book," the book that you are about to finish.

Around the World by Freighter was essentially complete when I walked down *Manet's* gangplank. Some polishing of the edges and a final review were all that remained before the CD was sent to the publisher. I hope that I have created a work that will answer Marise's questions and be of interest to others.

For the potential freighter traveler I simply say, if I could do it without this book, you are now far more prepared than I, go for it. For the inquiring mind of any age, I would like to think that somewhere in these pages is a spark that will ignite your further interest. For the armchair traveler, you have traveled around the world sitting down, a claim worthy of Guinness. Congratulations to you all.

For the past twelve weeks it has been an effort to record each day's events without sacrificing pleasures of the trip. At the same time it has been a daily joy to interpret and shape activities in my mind, then give birth to them on a blank computer screen. I hope you have enjoyed your journey through my maternity ward.

About the Author
By the Author
Unfortunately my biographer took the day off. Not having anyone to describe me in glowing terms, I will attempt an honest self-examination.

I am an ordinary guy with an extraordinary wife. Together we have raised two superior children who in turn have raised four superb grandchildren. I had a mediocre job as a civil engineer with the State of New York for too long. I have average interests which don't include sports, movies, or golf and I don't particularly like to sit around and chat.

All in all, I'm a dull guy with one major flaw. I have a bad habit of being curious, inquiring, inquisitive, and nosy. I like to know what, where, when, why, and especially, how much. I am also cheap.

If you also lack an interest in football, films, or friends, you might think about leaving on an extended trip around the world. You may enjoy your absence, as will your friends.

TO PURCHASE ADDITIONAL

COPIES OF THIS BOOK,

PLEASE VISIT:

http://www.trafford.com/robots/04-1054.html

FOR COPIES OF:

CARE TO JOIN ME?
DAY BY DAY ON THE APPALACHIAN TRAIL

Also by Bob Hartley
Visit: http://www.trafford.com/robots/03-1508.html

Thoughts about either book may be sent to:
www.info@Trafford.com